AURA MASTERY

"I believe, Johannes is opening up the understanding of the human energy fields that make up our spiritual-mental selves. This work is definitely the way of healing in the next millennium. Read this book."

Dannion Brinkley,
Author #1 New York Bestseller "Saved by the Light"

"I have been searching for a breakthrough device such as this since I first got involved in biofeedback research in 1969. I think the Inneractive Aura Video Station and AURA MASTERY will prove to be an invaluable tool for anyone interested in knowing themselves, or in helping others to manifest greater health and well being. It is an obvious choice for health professionals who can now demonstrate and more accurately determine the efficiency of their work."

Steven Halpern,
Recording artist, producer and author

"You will love this book. Practice AURA MASTERY and you will see tremendous changes in your life."

Bettina Bernoth, author of "Magical Auras"

AURA MASTERY

AURA MASTERY is a very simple and powerful program to see yourself and your environment as "bundles of information and energy" and to change your own Energy and Vibration to a higher level.

These are the basic AURA MASTERY GUIDELINES:

● **INCREASE YOUR ENERGY**

Do things in your daily life, which will increase your physical, emotional, mental and spiritual energies? Change or eliminate activities, which drain your energy or create negativity or stress.

● **RAISE YOUR VIBRATION**

Increase your vibration to create more beauty and love in your life and to go to a higher level of perfection and consciousness. Look into yourself and live to the best of your abilities.

This book is published by:

Inneractive • 520 Washington Blvd. # 907
Marina del Rey, CA 90292 • U.S.A
Phone: 310-390-7090 • Fax: 310-390-8167
E-mail: aura@inneractive.com
Internet: http://www.inneractive.com

© 1998 copyright by Johannes R. Fisslinger

Printed in the U.S.A
ISBN 0-9651531-0-X

Aura-in-motion, Aura Video Station, Your Aura Video, Inneractive, Bio Glove, AURA MASTERY are trademarks of Inneractive USA.

Excerpted from LIFE COLORS © 1991 by Pamala Oslie. Reprinted with permission of New World Library, San Rafael, CA 94903.

Any information offered here if acted on is intended to be adjunctive to the advice and care of a physician or other trusted health professionals. All Inneractive programs or products are not intended and/or are not a substitute for proper medical or therapeutic care. If you have any physical, emotional or mental problems please consult a trained health professional.

TABLE OF CONTENTS

ACKNOWLEDGEMENTS

I am forever grateful to the multitude of these gracious and wonderful people for the support, understanding and caring they have expressed over the last several years. I feel extremely blessed to have met so many interesting and passionate individuals.

I am even more grateful for the opportunity to be able to live out my own dream. To live this creative, interesting life and to fulfill my visions and innermost life goals would truly be insignificant if I could not share and enjoy them with my close friends and family.

To my wife Bettina, one of my greatest teachers. I have learned so much from her, especially the indispensable art of communicating and sharing my innermost feelings. I love you.

I am equally and consciously grateful for my wonderful parents. Having the opportunity to grow up in the country with such freedom, openness and peace was indeed a tremendous gift for me. I also need to thank, with the deepest appreciation, my sister Jutta, my brother Helmut and all my friends and relatives in my hometown in good, old Bavaria, Germany.

To Montie and Jerry for their programming work and for their technical skills and support in developing Inneractive technology.

To Sunshine, Alana, Jeremy and all Inneractive friends around the world for their support in promoting Inneractive Aura Video technology and AURA MASTERY.

To Dannion Brinkley for his message and his ability to be a powerful and loving spiritual being.

To Steven Halpern, my favorite New Age Musician, for his wonderful healing music and for writing the foreword to this book.

To Dr. Richard Johnson, one of the pioneers in the field of Biofeedback and Mind/Body healing, for his support.

To Pamala Oslie for her book Life Colors.

To Gene for editing this book.

To Rositta, Bela, Anton and Cornelia, who supported me all these years, Thank you for everything.

It is imperative that I also thank all my teachers and spiritual guides who throughout the years have helped me shape my abilities, skills and knowledge. They have each been more than instrumental in helping me find my vision, my inner trust and my own belief.

Special thanks must also be extended to all my friends and the people who have supported me through the years, including: Sarvesh - I love your magic, Martina, Govinda, Dietmar, Beat, Scott, David, Anna, Laurie, and ...

To every other living being who is willing to guide and support humanity and our planet into a new era of growth, prosperity and consciousness.

FOREWORD

For thousands of years, people around the world have known and honored the power of music to affect Body, Mind and Spirit. Music makes us feel good, energized, it can be relaxing or uplifting. Such music can literally "tune" our human instrument.

Other music stresses us, irritates us and weakens us, literally knocking us "out of tune".

Until recently, researchers relied primarily upon broad physiological measurements or subjective verbal responses from listeners to try to identify the effects of a selection of music. Many of its effects are too subtle to measure by traditional scientific devices.

Up until now, there has never been a way to observe the instantaneous, real-time effects of music on our subtle energy fields - our aura - which affords the most comprehensive and holistic picture yet. The aura is dynamic, and much more responsive and informative, in living color, than any snapshot could ever be.

Matching the right music to the right use can help you maximize the benefits you want to receive, especially if you are looking for music to help you relax, meditate, or amplify your body's self-healing energies.

Why is music so important?

Language gives us a clue. Concepts like 'being in harmony' and 'being in tune' are fundamental to music, as they are now also acknowledged to 'sound health' and overall well being.

Every atom, molecule, cell and gland vibrates at a characteristic frequency and radiates and resonates with sound at a specific frequency. Using the right music can provide a form of 'sound nourishment'. You might think of it as 'vitamins of the airwaves'. But in this case, the vitamins are pure energy, not slowed-down to dense physical matter.

For the many people, listening to music that evokes an alpha brain wave response is the easiest way to achieve a sense of inner peace and relaxation. It can actually put you in harmonic resonance and entrainment with the dominant energy field of the earth itself!

Many of the devices currently on the market, however, do not support this entrainment process of music. They tend to take the listener out of the desired state as it operates.

Not so with the Inneractive Aura Video Station: in fact, it is exactly the opposite. Watching your Aura Color image as you listen to music can actually enhance and amplify the benefits of music.

I have been searching for a breakthrough device such as this since I first got involved in biofeedback research in 1969. I think the Inneractive Aura Video Station and AURA MASTERY will prove to be an invaluable tool for anyone interested in knowing themselves, or in helping others to manifest greater health and well being. It is an obvious choice for health professionals who can now demonstrate and more accurately determine the efficiency of their work.

I am delighted to have been invited to help introduce the work of a true creative genius, Johannes R. Fisslinger.

For sound health,

Steven Halpern
Recording artist, producer and author

PREFACE

Understanding the connection between our body, mind and energy is essential not only to our well being but also our personal and spiritual growth. We know, our society is interconnected, computers are interconnected, families are interconnected, humans are interconnected with each other, and every single human being is interconnected within him or herself. It is impossible to escape or negate this fact.

Mind/body connection means that we are a complex, interconnected, living system. Our physical body, with its countless components and systems, is interconnected with our emotions, feelings, thoughts, values, beliefs, intuitions and equally important, our higher mind. Actually, it is not only a mind/body connection, but actually a mind/body unity. Mind and body are only different expressions of the same unit. This concept and knowledge constitutes the basis for our work.

The AURA VIDEO STATION and AURA MASTERY were developed to display your mind/body interactivity reflected through your own life energy or aura. They are tools designed for the purpose of assisting you in exploring and healing your Inner World of Mind, Body and Energy.

AURA MASTERY, simply defined, means interactive mind/body and energy feedback. It literally opens a wondrous window into your own self and reflects your inner beauty and radiance. The mind/body connection is demystified, made practical and accessible for all human beings.

Inneractive Aura Video technology displays your mind/body and energy connection and the AURA MASTERY program gives you the necessary feedback and tools to make the changes in your life which you always wanted to create in the first place.

If you change your Inner World,
The Outer World will follow.

The thousands of people around the world who came in contact with and have practiced AURA MASTERY techniques will agree with me, that the moment you honestly decide to take action, and the moment you change inside, your environment around you will change dramatically and accordingly.

I personally invite you to join others just like you and me to make the next step, called AURA MASTERY - the step of mastering our own life, living our full potential now, and creating our dreams and visions today.

Yours sincerely,

Johannes R. Fisslinger

INTRODUCTION

Some time ago while reading Dannion Brinkley's book "Saved by the Light" and James Redfield's book "The Celestine Prophecy", I found myself completely surprised. I thought it was incredible that books filled with information which relate to human life energy, insights into human behavior and spiritual growth, could be number one on The New York Times bestseller list for more than a year. It occurred to me that the only explanation for this incredible phenomenon is that there is a tremendous demand in all of us to expand our limited perceptions about both life and ourselves. We are beginning to know it is time for all of us to connect with our higher powers and live to our full potential.

Another wonderful book which has touched me deeply is, "Timeless Mind, Ageless Body", by Deepak Chopra. In this and his other groundbreaking books, Mr. Chopra clearly explains that we all have to understand our own energetic nature. We are both information and energy combined and therefore need to act and live accordingly.

After reading the above books and working with thousands of people myself, I began to wonder if there was an easy but accurate way to measure or verify our energetic nature. We are indeed information and energy but how can we create the technology which will help us to understand and practice the above principles? Wouldn't it be easier for most of us to make positive changes in our lives if we had a "visual tool" or a supportive instruments which could give us honest feedback with reference to where we are right now and what is going on inside of us?

There are many people who have read hundreds of books, participated in countless courses and practiced many different techniques, without really achieving the results they were hoping for and expecting.

I have posed this question to many people: What have you actually done to take control and master your own life after reading books like "The Celestine Prophecy" or "Timeless Mind, Ageless Body"? In order to achieve the results we all desire we need to integrate mind/body concepts into our daily life.

It became clear to me that AURA MASTERY, which I was in the process of developing at that time, will unquestionably be the next step for countless people to take after reading about and understanding the principles of mind, body and energy.

Inner growth requires real change and cannot be achieved by just reading or participating in activities of a mental nature. Real change can only take place when we change our mind, our emotions and our body and create awareness in our life.

AURA MASTERY is a continues training and exploration program to discover, explore and heal our Inner World of Mind, Body and Energy. It will help you to increase your energy level and to raise your vibration to create more beauty and love in your life.

AURA MASTERY is a journey into yourself. A journey of exploration and discovery.

MY EXPERIENCES WITH ENERGY AND COLORS

During my research, studies and work with Inneractive AURA MASTERY and Aura Imaging Technology, I have had the opportunity to meet many healers and various other people who have the ability to see or perceive the human energy field. My experience was that the aura colors and patterns, which were measured using Inneractive technology, were extremely close in proximity to the colors clairvoyants perceived around human subjects.

Over the last five years I have conducted various and extensive experiments which verify this phenomena. For example, we would set up a test situation in which clairvoyants would look at an individual and describe what colors they see around them. The clairvoyants would also describe for us certain personality traits, behavioral patterns and belief systems from that same person. At the same time I would verify the described information through the use of Biofeedback Imaging equipment. In most cases the clairvoyant would see the same or very similar colors in the human energy field that we measured and displayed on our monitors. Also, through interviews, the test person could verify their own personality traits, which are connected with certain aura colors or with life energy colors.

Several years ago I had the pleasure of having a number of long distance phone conversations with Pamala Oslie, a well-known clairvoyant and author of the book, "Life Colors". Reading Pamala's book served to convince me that she not only had the wonderful gift of perceiving the human energy field, but was also able to understand its far reaching implications. In her book she describes in great detail the connection of the various aura colors she perceives and their correlation with certain personality traits, emotional, mental and spiritual behavior.

During this time I was deeply embedded in a transitional period in my own life. First, I was just at the tail end, the downside, of a five year long relationship. Second, I wasn't sure or clear if I should continue with a successful business I had established in Europe. Third, and most important at the time, I felt a general discomfort with pretty much everything I was doing.

I decided I needed a vacation, a little rest and relaxation. When I arrived in Los Angeles from Munich, Germany I instantly felt a lightness and an easiness which seemed to consume me. I loved the sunny climate. It felt wonderful, recharging and refreshing.

I rented a convertible for a few days and made my way up the coast to Santa Barbara. I had known Pam only from our phone conversations but when I met her in person I immediately sensed a very light energy which seemed to be all around her. The instant she saw me she said, "I knew it. I knew you'd be a Violet-Yellow."

" Sounds good to me," I replied, "And but just what exactly does that mean?"

She smiled warmly as she mentioned that a person radiating Violet-Yellow colors is usually playful, spiritual, sensitive, independent and motivated by dreams and creative ideas. I returned the smile with the realization that she had clearly described the way I normally felt.

I received a wonderful reading as well as valuable, personal counseling from Pam. She told me one of the things I had to do was to fulfill a vision in this particular lifetime, which the violet color reflects. On the other hand, I was also destined to enjoy life, have fun and express myself in a playful way.

Interestingly enough at that time in my life, violet and yellow were the most predominant aura colors on all of my Aura Photos or Aura Videos.

During one of our many conversations Pam also asked me if I was aware that Southern California was known for both it's Yellow and Violet-Yellow personalities. Actually, I had experienced that feeling before but couldn't formulate either how or why.

But whenever I was in Southern California I felt uplifted, light and creative. Pam shared a great deal of good information with me along with advice on specific areas through her readings of my energy field.

She could sense or see things and situations that were connected both to my past experiences and to my future. One statement she made struck me very deeply. She said that if I wanted to fulfill my vision and my ideas in this lifetime, I needed to be more powerful, more centered and more focused.

I had a tendency of being too scattered, wanting to do too many projects at once (very typical for Violets), and my Yellow personality aspect didn't want to commit to hard, long-lasting plans or visions. She suggested that I both wear and try to attract more Dark-Green qualities in my life.

My initial reaction was remarkably negative. I truly dislike the heavy feeling I sense when I even think of dark green or emerald green. It was an uncomfortable feeling and I didn't feel a particular need for these qualities in my life. Dark green sounded too serious, too grounded, too depressing.

After a few relaxing and wonderful days in Santa Barbara and Los Angeles I left California and went back to Germany. During the trip I gave great deal of thought to the connection of colors with certain personality traits, emotions and thought patterns. I could definitely see a strong connection in my life, but what on earth did she mean when she mentioned dark green would be good for me.

My mind drifted back seven or eight years ago, back to the beginning when I first started to work with bio-energy, healing, alternative therapies and colors. At that time I wasn't very grounded. Some people even considered me spacy. There was a time where I didn't even like to confront myself with the real world. Everything seemed to be too hard, too insensitive, too brutal, too unspiritual. I found myself filled with unanswerable questions.

Why are people like this? Why can't people just be nice and supportive with each other? I saw cutthroat competition, disturbances and negativity nearly everywhere I looked. I was going through an intense personal and spiritual transformation.

Some time later when I saw Aura Imaging Photography for the first time and made my first aura photo, I was not surprised at seeing many Violet-White colors surrounding myself. These high vibration colors seemed to represent my inner experience and my life very well.

Later in my life I could always see the connection between the colors I loved to wear and the ones I saw on my aura imaging photos and their correlation with my inner psychological or emotional situation. But why should I wear or create Dark Green color qualities in my life? I just didn't get it. Somehow, someway, I knew Pam was right, but I could not fully understand the implication involved.

Then an incredible thing happened. After being back in Germany for awhile I met a wonderful woman. When I saw her first aura photo I was truly surprised. She had a very harmonious, solid and balanced looking, deep green color in her energy field. Our relationship blossomed and after a few months, I found to my greater surprise, that this deep-green color had begun to appear in my own energy field. I was beginning to understand what deep green meant for me.

A few months later, through my own aura imaging photos and inner experiences using meditations and exercises, I noticed a change in my life energy field. More and more green was beginning to appear. This was surprising to me because until this occurred I didn't perceive or barely noticed any green colors at all.

I consciously wondered if my girlfriend and our new relationship really did all that to me. I questioned if I was slave of my relationships or was it a natural process, connected somehow with the universal energy flow.

After a while I began to notice subtle changes in my behavior, my emotions, my feelings and also in my thought processes. I could sense myself becoming more balanced, more relaxed, more integrated in my body. I could actually feel my heart opening up, being forced to communicate more than I wanted to at an earlier point in my life.

Another year passed by and I decided it was finally time for me to move to Southern California. As usual, this decision was very intuitive. By this time I was confronted with Green and Deep-Green qualities. I started giving lectures and workshops and my communication changed radically toward speaking more clearly about my own truth and expressing my feelings more directly without holding anything in reserve. I could feel my heart opening up and my physical body became much more powerful but also more relaxed. My thinking processes took on a new degree of clarity and I was now able to make precise plans and see them through to fruition. The Deep Green color seemed to have a very balancing influence in my life.

After living in Southern California for some time now I can clearly understand why so many Yellow and Violet-Yellow personalities are drawn here. This area offers everything these personalities are seeking: year round sunshine, miles and miles of beaches, beautiful people, easy living, visionary, futuristic thinking, being ahead of its time, and a seemingly endless source of new ideas and technologies. It is also the entertainment capitol of the world, educating, transforming and stimulating humanity in many ways and areas.

AURA AND ENERGY

AURA MASTERY uses certain scientific and spiritual basics as a foundation. It is not necessary to know or even agree with this information for an individual to effectively practice AURA MASTERY. It is only given so you can be mentally satisfied, understand what you are doing and be aware of our basic premise. It will be easier for you to understand some of the concepts in this book if you are aware of the following basics, which we use as our foundation.

- Mind, Body and Spirit are interconnected energetic systems. You as a conscious person are the operator.
- We are bundles of information and energy in a vast universe of information and energy.
- Einstein proved and Science knows "All matter is energy".
- Religious and spiritual teachers have told us for centuries that we are beings of energy - light.
- Scientific research of the human body over the last decades has proven that we are energetic in nature.
- Our Life Energy is the link between Mind, Body and Spirit.
- Awareness is the key to understand and master your life.
- Taking conscious responsibility for your life is the first step to create a spiral upward toward well being, healing and growth.

If you are interested in theoretical explanations or scientific background I refer you to many of my colleagues. In the reference section I have mentioned several interesting books you should consider reading. I especially recommend Deepak Chopra, Dr. Richard L Johnson, Barbara Brennan, Dr. Richard Gerber and Dr. Robert O. Becker. I find these authors to be important because of the extensive research they have conducted in mind/body interaction and the energetic and electro-magnetic nature of man.

INTERACTIVE WORLD, INNERACTIVE PEOPLE

We live in a wondrous time where both information and energy are important aspects in our daily life. The next revolution of our species, which has already clearly begun, is commonly referred to as the information or electronic age. It is virtually impossible to imagine a world without such technological marvels as television sets, computers, electricity, telephones and fax machines. We use these wonderful inventions of the 20th century in our daily life without giving much thought to it.

Through this explosive growth and the development of various technologies our planet has become much smaller then it used to be. We find ourselves in a shrinking world, which is interconnected in many areas and many fields. Technology and consciousness have evolved over the last few decades to the point where interactivity is understood and used both in practical applications and in our daily life. To know you can contact a friend or business associate on the other side of the planet just by dialing through your phone, fax or modem has created a tremendous closeness. The Super Information Highway, or Internet, demonstrates the desire of people all over the world to interact with each other, to share experiences and to live as one, global society on our home planet earth.

We have also grown to accept the fact that we are interconnected with our environment. We are all breathing the same air and drinking the same water. We are living in an environment, which is changing dramatically, making us all aware that radioactivity or smog does not stop at one countries border. Science tells us we are made out of the same atoms, units of information and energy, living in a vast universe of information and energy. We are living on an interactive planet earth, sharing a similar heritage and history. We are a global family.

AURA MASTERY realizes that every single person is connected with their own, individual environment, with nature and the people with whom they share their life. Inneractivity, in simple terms, means we are interconnected with all people and we share an inner connection each with the other.

But we are not only interconnected outside ourselves on a global scale. If we look inside we will find a vast universe, which is virtually unexplored. The adventure of exploring our inner world of mind, body and spirit is perhaps the largest and most important challenge a human being can face. Our inner world is interconnected with our outer reality.

Computers are interactively connected with each other through the Internet. People are Inneractively connected through their own InnerNet. Within ourselves we can discover an incredible and exciting world, an inner network of information and energy. If you are interested in perceiving and understanding your own Inneractivity, then you have to start within.

Let's start to explore Inneractive AURA MASTERY and the relationship between Mind, Body and Energy further.

AURA MASTERY 1:

Stop reading for a minute. Try to sit or lie as comfortable as possible, making sure your spine is straight and your body is relaxed. Take a deep breath in, expand your belly and your chest and let go completely while you slowly exhale.

Feel or touch your physical body. You have just read that your physical, mechanical body is of great importance to you. Feel your feet, you spine, your head, all working together. Feel your muscles, your organs or go even deeper into your cells and atoms. They all belong to your mechanical body.

And, there is another part of you, which is as real as your physical body. Feel your emotions, the energy-in-motion moving through your body. In your belly you might feel a sense of power, strength and activity. Take a deep breath into your heart, allow it to open and feel the tremendous love dwelling within you.

You can't touch these emotions, yet they are there. Like clouds of energy they are within you or around you.

Now, focus your attention inside your head. What kinds of thoughts come to your mind? Do you think about this exercise or about what you have read a minute ago? Watch each thought or thought process pass by like clouds in the sky. They come and they go.

If you can watch your thoughts come and go then you can't be your thoughts, can you? You are the watcher of your thoughts; you are the intelligence behind everything.

Please stops reading now, close your eyes go through the above process of feeling your physical, mechanical body and your energetic, timeless body. Try to stay in this expanded state of awareness for a few minutes

ARE WE HUMAN BIO-COMPUTERS?

A simple analogy with a computer will show how we, as human beings, function and interact with the world around us.

Body	=	Hardware
Mind	=	Software
Spirit	=	Programmer

You might ask yourself, are we really human bio-computers?

Well, we find similar principals and functions of existence in a computer unit as we do in human beings. The computer hardware, with all its electrical wires, currents, relay stations, etc. can easily be compared with the human physical body. In a Computer you will find a motherboard which functions as the equivalent of the human brain.

You will find wires and circuitry, which run through the complete system connecting all of the various parts with each other. This could be compared to the nervous system in a human being.

Computer hardware consists of different levels of density and materials, starting from silicon and iron to plastic and electricity to micro currents. Naturally, a computer is only a poor copy of a functioning human but you can already see the similarities between the basic structure of a computer and that of a human body.

Without a physical body or the human hardware we couldn't act, move or literally do anything within the 3-dimensional and physical world. We would be limited to non-physical actions. If we have a solid and equally strong super model of a physical body/hardware, we will be able to achieve more, function better and act faster. Weak or slow hardware does not really support us in our work or in our life.

However, we can't just throw our hardware away and replace it with a new one. Even though medicine and science are now ingeniously able to replace many parts of our physical hardware system, I strongly believe we need to understand our interconnectedness - our Mind-Body-Spirit connection - if we want to create dynamic and lasting changes in our physical body.

We can find many similarities between the human mind and the various software programs, which are used to drive computers. Our mind has a variance of emotional structures and behavioral systems, which operate much, like a software program.

Both the mechanized software and our mind decide what type of actions will be taken under certain sets of circumstances. They each give clear and precise instructions as to what is supposed to happen as a result of information, which is input or received.

Different software programs, and conversely, different minds, understandably create different actions or results.

There are striking similarities between computer software and the human mind. A specific part of each of our minds is responsible for organization and structuring, another is designated separately for all counting functions and even another part for the sole purpose of communicating. But our mind is clearly and most certainly not limited to basic, analytical thinking and other similar processes. Our mind is capable of the greatest of all gifts: creativity, the ability to create new, challenging and exciting ideas, which seem to come from nowhere.

We can be both intuitive and imaginative by using our higher mind for the purposes of creation and creativity. While this, in and of itself, is miraculous, there's even more. The human mind is equally capable of perceiving and also transmitting feelings and emotions. Feelings of passion, love and also compassion are felt by every human being not only through their mind but also in their physical body. This indicates clearly and sends a rather significant message that the mind is strongly connected with the physical body. E-motions = energy in motion, seems to be an integrated and very powerful part of the human mind/body.

Both our mind and software found in a computer have to be programmed or they cease to function properly. The good news is that at any given time, with the proper tools and effort, they are both capable of being reprogrammed. The most important point to know is how to change a software program in that same computer and or in our own mind.

The question we have to ask ourselves, is the mind or the software program the final step, the ultimate. Quite obviously it is not. Which simply means we need to find the programmer, the creator, to answer any and all of our questions.

It is a simple matter of fact that a computer is basically and intrinsically stupid unless and until someone gives it life or meaning. A computer can only fulfill the functions it is told to do.

The programmer decides through various software applications what functions and abilities the computer has to fulfill. He has designed, structured and programmed his software for specific purposes or functions.

It is not uncommon for computer users to occasionally feel that the computer they are using knows virtually everything or has an intelligence of its own. But in reality it is the programmer of the software who gave the program its own specific qualities. In essence he was the one who gave it life. He alone decided what tools, instruments and instructions it would take to perform and fulfill the various and specific functions.

Today, we will each think the same thoughts, experience the same emotions and have the same belief patterns that we did yesterday, the day before yesterday, and the day before that. These thoughts, beliefs and emotions are based in and emanate from our subconscious and superconscious mind and directly create and direct our future.

The human aura is considered to be the field of energy, which contains all our information past, present and future. In understanding our Aura Colors we begin to reprogram our mind, body and spirit.

If we experience thoughts and emotions, we need to ask ourselves, who is the experiencer of the thought or emotion? Who is the thinker of the thought? Who is the decision maker and the choice maker? If we are able to watch and observe our body as well as our mind, it follows logically that there has to be something beyond mind/body which we might call spirit.

We as powerful, spiritual beings, individually create and design all of our own programs. Every minute of every day and night, while awake and while sleeping, we are designing and programming our own mind and our own body. Often many of us think we are the program itself or that we have no control over our emotional and mental processes. But who else is better able to change our mind than each of us as individuals.

If we are fully aware of our mind/body connection we will understand that we are indeed the programmer or choice maker in our life and that awareness is the primary key to this process. Spirit or awareness is the essential key to our personal and our spiritual growth.

MECHANICAL AND ENERGETIC BODY

Another example, or concept, will help us understand the dynamic connection of mind, body, spirit and energy.

Over the last few centuries we have held the belief that we are indeed a physical body which lives in a physical universe. This old, mechanical paradigm is not necessarily wrong, it is only limited in its perception. We have a physical body, which is made of atoms, cells and organs. Our physical body is bound by time and space and driven by biochemical processes.

Quantum physics tells us that matter is energy. If you look at the behavior of an atomic particle you will recognize its twofold nature. These subatomic units sometimes behave as particles and at other times as waves.

This means we are not only physical and solid but also energetic. In essence we are living simultaneously in two worlds.

Our quantum mechanical body consists of our thoughts, emotions, feelings, beliefs, memories, etc., and is not bound by space and time. This energetic "body" is often referred to as the Aura - a pulsating field of information and energy, which expands far beyond the limitations of our physical body.

Both worlds interact with each other. Our physical, mechanical and our energetic, subtle body are an interconnected system in which we as conscious beings are both the operator and the programmer.

The moment we recognize and remember that we are in charge of our own destiny, that we are the ultimate creators of our own reality, we can take full responsibility and action. We design and program our mind-software the way we want for very specific purposes and reasons. We are the creator of our own mind-software program.

The Aura Video Station can proof our multi-dimensional nature. By measuring the energetic flow in the body we can show how our emotions and thoughts can influence and change our physical body and the state of consciousness we are in.

On the other hand changing our Aura will influence our reality - the way we perceive and live our life. This process is called AURA MASTERY, the ability to change and master our Aura through the power of our mind.

THE HUMAN ENERGY FIELD

"He is radiating an aura of power and success."
"She has the charisma of a spiritual leader"

Statements like the above clearly indicate we have grown to accept the fact that all individuals, all the time, are constantly expressing a certain radiance, an aura, which is completely unique to our own personalities. But we seldom consider this radiance to be an actual, existing energy field emanating from our physical body. Even so, virtually every single one of us has experienced the feeling of this power or subtle radiation, which transpires from certain individuals.

But it is not only our own perceptions, which indicate that auric fields exist. There are countless descriptions of clairvoyants, people who are capable of perceiving or actually seeing the human energy field. Some of these sensitive and gifted individuals have proven again and again that they indeed have the ability to perceive a higher dimension of existence.

Many scientists from all around the world have also researched these phenomena. Dr. Valerie Hunt electronically measured both the frequency and the location of the bio-field on hundreds of human subjects. Her readings directly correlated with results received from established aura readers.

Between 1970 and 1990, Hiroshi Motoyama electronically measured the acupuncture meridians which span thousands of years of eastern medicine. Dr. Robert Becker also verified the existence of a human electro-magnetic field. He discovered direct, current control systems on the human body, which change with the state of health and disease.

Throughout history, many different names and descriptions have been given to the human life energy field around us. Depending on their cultural background, various scientists and other individuals have referred to this energy field as: biofield, orgon, electro-magnetic field, life force, chi, vital energy or aura.

But at this point I don't wish to look into this subject from a scientific point of view. In our interactions with other people we are continually confronted with the effects of the human energy field. Attraction or rejection are just some of the feelings we experience when we come in contact with other people.

The subtle, auric field, which radiates around us reflects our inner world. Whatever we feel, think or believe inside, is reflected within our aura and radiates and interacts with our environment.

Could this possibly be the reason why some people always seem to have good luck in their life while others seem to have none? And why is it that some people seem to attract the same life situations over and over?

I am sure you know or at least have heard of the type woman who left her partner because he abused her. But shortly thereafter, as if some magical attraction radiates around her, she meets another person. In the beginning of their relationship this person is attentive and caring. But then, and usually after a short period of time, she discovers he is as violent and abusive as her former boyfriend. Perhaps you have seen reoccurring patterns like these in your own life.

We have all experienced this attraction - reaction phenomena. For me personally it is especially obvious when I 'm in a bad mood. I may look completely normal, certainly not angry at all. But for some unexplained reason my mood and emotions seem to radiate around me and other people pick up on them. I find it fascinating how many angry people or strange situations I can attract if I am angry myself. But luckily, if I'm in a very positive, flowing life situation, I also express an aura of luck and success which opens countless doors and lets the best of things happen virtually effortlessly.

AURA MASTERY 2:

After you have prepared yourself for this exercise, close you eyes and take a few deep breaths. Focus your attention inside your physical body. Feel or imagine organs such as your skin, your heart, your liver or your intestines. These physical parts of your body are solid and easy to locate.

Now it is time to go beyond your physical body. Imagine your physical body to be a balloon, a balloon with the outlines of your body. Feel the air that moves within this balloon. Feel the different areas, the difference in pressure or intensity inside your balloon of energy. You might also notice that some areas within your balloon are lighter or darker. Go through your whole body and spot the light and dark areas. Your head might feel heavy and tense, your left chest open and sensitive or your lower back might feel blocked.

Now you know that your energy balloon has variations. After you have finished this body scan it is time to expand your balloon beyond the outlines of your physical body. Just imagine someone blowing air or energy into you. This fresh and recharging energy feels remarkably refreshing, not unlike a high feeling you might experience at a beach or mountain.

While you breathe in, feel your energy balloon expand and recharge. Without doing or forcing anything, your balloon of energy will get bigger and bigger. You feel a lightness and a happiness come over you. The more your energy balloon expands the lighter and energized you feel.

For several minutes allow this expansion of your energy to happen. Breathing in will expand and recharge you, breathing out allows you to feel the lightness and the beauty within. After some time you can check how big your energy balloon is. Did it expand a few inches around your physical body or did it expand several feet? Also be aware if you feel lighter, more energized or more balanced within your energy balloon.

You can use this exercise in any situation during the day. Sit back for a minute and allow your body to recharge himself. Fill your energy field with fresh and strong energy, with lightness and love.

OUR LIFE ENERGY BATTERY

".... President Clinton with an aura of power and..."
"...President Clinton, recharging his political energies in the
rural counties where he began his career..."
Los Angeles Times, April 95

The above quotes sound strangely to me as if the President of the United States somehow has an aura and an integrated system of inner batteries which he is able to recharge at will. Perhaps that's one of the advantages of being a president!

Fortunately, for all of us, it's not only presidents who have a battery for their energy. We all possess a life energy battery of our own.

On occasion I will find I have no energy left for work or anything else. Once I am in an empty energy state I have to recharge myself either through sleeping, eating good, healthy and energizing food, jogging, playing volleyball, relaxing in my Jacuzzi, listening to good music, meditating, making love or many other recharging activities. I am sure you have experienced this feeling as well. The question to be asked is, do you know what activities are recharging for you, or do you have difficulty in filling up your batteries again?

We all know and understand that virtually every device we use in our daily life needs some form of energy to function properly. We either decide to connect those devices to a central electricity system such as power lines, which connect single households, or to a local energy source such as a battery. Most of the appliances or toys we use come not only with instructions on what power source to use but also how to recharge them.

But did you receive instructions about your energy source and how to recharge your own life energy batteries? I know I didn't. Have you ever even thought about your own power source? Where do you get your energy from?

Is it in your own hands to recharge yourself or do you need somebody or something else to do it for you? You might say to yourself, good questions, but why are they important? After all, I live a relatively good life without thinking about recharging myself. I haven't had any serious or life threatening problems so far.

And, you would definitely be correct with that attitude. Whether you are aware of your life energy or not, your life energy batteries recharge without any conscious effort. For the most part this is primarily an autonomous body process, which doesn't need any of your attention for it to work. It just does. Knowing and understanding this simple but unchallengable fact brings about an even larger question.

How is it that some people seem to have tremendous, unlimited energy available? How is it that certain, strong personalities know how to recharge their batteries in order to live a more successful, fulfilling and prosperous life? Why do you sometimes feel completely empty and don't know where or how to get the energy to achieve and fulfill your desires, goals or dreams?

Why are some people always healthy and energetic while others are often sick and powerless? Do you want to be dependent on other people or situations for your circumstances and your life or are you willing to be independently responsible for this process?

Wouldn't it be much better, for you and for everyone whose lives you touch, if you would be in charge of your own life energy battery recharging process?

Inneractive AURA MASTERY will teach you to be a master in recharging your own life energy batteries. As an energetic and vibrant person you will have more than enough energy and strength available to fulfill not only your own personal dreams but also to help others live better lives.

All too often we fail to fully understand the concept of energy and how we can easily learn to recharge and revitalize ourselves.

But there is much more to it. Not only do we have energy available in our daily lives; we are beings of energy. The sum of our very existence is energy. Religion has repeatedly told us this for thousands of years and science has proven this to be a fact in this century. But how does this knowledge affect each of us in our own reality? Is it significant both in and to our lives? Another stimulating question: Do we act and live like the beings of energy we know ourselves to be, or do we still continue to only exist as physical and mechanical beings?

It is time for every individual and our corresponding societies to accept the fact that not only do we have physical bodies, but that we are indeed beings of energy. Our very core is life energy. Once we come to understand this we then have to integrate this fact into our daily lives. Everything is energetic, in a constant flux and with non-stop movement. Energy can never be static.

Once we truly understand this, positive change and growth becomes a natural process. Resistance to change is counterproductive and serves only to drain our natural energy source. Once we begin to live as energy people we have the flexibility and strength to grow and expand into a new and exciting dimension of existence.

You will discover in the Inneractive AURA MASTERY and Aura Color Test that every person is completely individual and differs in their perceptions and beliefs. We experience our environment and life itself through very special glasses, the glasses of perception, beliefs and personality. While our perceptions may differ our essence is the same. We are units, bundles, or beings of energy in a highly unique form.

It is time for us to change our antiquated, out-of-date perceptions and accept the fact that we are energetic people - people composed of energy. We must learn to toss aside Darwinian beliefs and literally expand ourselves into something much higher and more evolved. To fully understand the concept of energy, we have to look deeper into the connection between Mind/Body, Energy and Colors.

COLOR TEST RESEARCH

During the research and development phase of AURA MASTERY and the Aura Video Station I wanted to get in contact with real people and real life situations. I wanted to discover if there was a correlation between colors and our personality or our current life situation. I decided to go to one location, a holistic fair, with the expectation of receiving some interesting and revealing results.

At this particular event I tested numerous participants as to which color they would select from a palate of twelve choices. They had to spontaneously make two choices without giving any thought to the process. The question posed was not what color they like to wear or what color they thought was best for them. Rather, the idea was to actually not choose, but to *feel* the colors and pick the ones, which caught their eyes.

What surprised me most, was that the majority of people chose the Lavender color first and Blue-Violet second. At that point I understood why psychic activities and phenomena are connected to Violet-Lavender colors. Actually, most of the psychics we measured and tested with the AURA VIDEO STATION vibrated in a Violet-Lavender color. But I never expected that nearly everyone who attended the event would select the same color.

The colors which people chose first and second in most standard color tests usually indicate the quality or vibration they are looking for. It reflects what they need at this moment in their life. It also reflects their longings and their desires.

The results of this event showed me what power our subconscious and superconscious mind plays in our day-to-day decision making process. Most people attended this event because they were somehow in need of the colors Violet-Lavender. They needed these qualities in their life. New ideas, ideals, inspiration, intuition, spiritual and psychic energies and healing are associated with Lavender-Violet colors. Other equally important things would include fantasy, dreams and an escape from reality.

Choosing Lavender as their first color showed their unconscious intention to face the above mentioned qualities.

Colors can give us valuable information about our current "inner" condition and can also be a powerful tool to achieve self-healing and personal growth. The more we become conscious about ourselves, the more we will become conscious about colors and their effects on our mind/body and spirit.

AURA MASTERY 3:

Try this as an experiment: The next time you go out, wear a color you don't like at all. For example, if you normally dress in black, blue or other dark colors, choose a bright color such as a strong red or bright yellow. Even if you don't like these colors at all I am sure you will always find an acceptable shade of this color.

While you do this you should stay consciously aware of what is happening to both yourself and the environment around you.

Examine your environment and the people you meet. Do they react differently then you are used to or would normally expect? Ask yourself how you feel wearing different colors. Do you feel uncomfortable wearing specific colors or do you like to play around with different shades and hues and their effect on both yourself and your friends?

Here is a special tip for women: One evening go out wearing a bright red dress, something which might even be described as sexy. The next day try wearing a deep blue dress, which most people would consider to be businesslike. Believe me, not only will you enjoy yourself but you will also experience a remarkable difference.

COLORS AND THEIR EFFECT IN YOUR DAILY LIFE

You have probably noticed that different colors can create very profound and distinguishing effects. The fact of the matter is that the various colors you wear can influence your feelings or thoughts. I learned this lesson in a rather unusual way.

One summer evening, some time ago, I wasn't feeling very well. I was scheduled to give a lecture and I just didn't feel up to it. I couldn't really back out because there was a significant audience waiting, interested in what I had to say.

After taking a quick shower I stood in front of my closet, trying desperately to decide what to wear. From that moment and for the rest of my life I will never again complain about women who can't make a decision as to what color they want to wear. I stared blankly, nothing was right. First I tried a violet shirt, but the moment I put it on I just felt very strange.

I was concerned to the point of telling my girlfriend something was wrong with me. I don't like my violet shirt anymore. Then I tried a yellow one, then a blue one. Nothing was even close to being satisfactory. I tried black trousers, gray trousers, jeans, nothing seemed to work.

I almost became angry with myself, actually posing the question, "Am I acting like a woman now, standing in front of the mirror for what seems like an eternity, complaining I have nothing to wear and finally wearing what I originally started out with?" No, I silently and logically replied. That doesn't sound like me at all.

As my girlfriend laughed at my predicament she explained that the next time she needed two hours to dress I might be better off if I just stayed quiet and continued to understand why it takes a certain amount of time. From that day on I understood the true effect of the colors of the clothing I was wearing.

Colors have a strong effect on our feelings and emotions. The more sensitive we are, the more we will be aware of the power of colors. After much consternation I finally decided on brownish-gray trousers and a turquoise-green shirt.

Both colors supported me that day in my attempts to stay grounded and relaxed and also to more clearly communicate my precise thoughts and feelings.

ENERGY AND COLORS

"We are bundles of information and energy in an unlimited field of information and energy ..."

The whole universe and we as human beings consist of universal life energy. This energy is the basic "fuel" of life. This basic life energy may show up in different forms, variations and densities, but essentially everything that exists is made of life energy.

It is easier to understand the connection between Life Energy - Humans - Colors, if you can visualize the following picture:

All human beings are like rainbows. Light, or life energy, is flowing into our system to both feed us and give us life. We function as prisms, allowing that light to flow through us. Like in a prism, the clear, white light reveals the rainbow of its colors. The only difference between a prism and us is that we are living, breathing beings.

We have the free will and decision making ability to express whatever color we desire. We are not static but active and alive prisms. We are the decision-makers. Our awareness and attention determines the reality we experience. We have the freedom to tune into any vibration or quality. Our focus, thoughts, emotions and beliefs determine how we express and live our life energy. Our focus and attention also decides what color of the rainbow we will radiate in our life.

As human beings we decide what colors of the rainbow we express. Our awareness, our choices and our decisions will ultimately determine what type and quality of life we will live.

Therefore, the quality or reality of life we experience is reflected through our life energy colors. If we decide to live our life energy with power and action we will vibrate and radiate with Red energy. If we are intellectual or analytical we will find a Tan-Yellow or Green life energy color. The moment we tune ourselves into sensitive, artistic and visionary living we will express and radiate a Blue, Violet life energy color.

After continually hearing that everything is energy, you might logically ask yourself how energy is defined or described. What is the easiest, most useful and most practical way of distinguishing between different forms and qualities of energy?

It is often difficult to describe the qualities of energy. A scientist might prefer a numerical number for a certain frequency. A technically oriented person might say 400 manometer for a certain shade of the color Blue-Violet. But for general or educational use, I feel it is inappropriate to use complicated terms, terms, which have little or no meaning for the majority of us.

I have found that both colors and sound are excellent ways of expressing or determining various qualities of energy. I personally prefer colors to sound because in our information oriented society we are trained to be much more visual then auditive.

Colors are absolutely natural for all of us because we are born with a color awareness. In actuality, the less knowledge we accumulate, the easier it is to use colors from an intuitive and natural point of view.

If you see the color RED you immediately associate it with certain feelings, thoughts or life situations. Obviously these associations are subjective and vary widely from person to person.

But if you hear a certain sound, just one tone, or are told about a frequency of 700 nanometer, it is more than likely you would not know what to associate it with. You would probably lose the information contained because there was no clear reference.

This is not true with colors. Psychological studies have proven that colors not only reflect our psycho-emotional states but also have a tremendous impact on our behavior as well as our moods.

Colors also are able to distinguish between different qualities of energy. We know of millions of colors or color combinations as much as we know that there is a vast universe with undefinable energetic vibrations. Colors can tell us in a simple but powerful symbolic language about the quality or state of energy.

There are uncountable color combinations, but every single color is composed of light. There are countless expressions of energy, but we are light-energy.

AURA MASTERY 4:

In this exercise it is especially important that your spine is straight. Feel your whole body with its emotions and vibrations. Let the balloon of energy expand around your physical body forming a halo or egg shaped auric field around you.

You have read about being a human prism and now it is time to experience it. Imagine a soft, white light above your head. This white light represents the universal life energy, the highest, powerful spiritual energy. Once you feel or see this white light allow it to flow through the top of your head into your body. The crown chakra opens up and you visualize and feel white light flowing into you. First your head fills up, then your throat, shoulders, arms and the rest of your body including the legs and feet.

During this recharging process you will see or feel different colors within yourself. These various colors are expressions of the white light. Like in a prism the white light will reveal its many forms. Just know, that the white light will transform into whatever color quality you need at this particular time.

Like a river, this stream of energy comes into your head, moves through your whole body and leaves again through your feet into the ground.

To expand your experience even more, follow the path of energy and tune into the colors you have created. Like in a prism, a bright red, a balanced green or a deep blue might appear in front of your inner eye. Imagine the colors becoming more vivid, more clear and visible. You will see or feel the dance of colors. Feel the white light transforming you into a being of light and colors.

LIFE ENERGY AND PERSONALITY TRAITS

Since 1990 I have had the opportunity to travel throughout the world and to come into contact with many Vibrational Healing practitioners and clairvoyants. Some of these highly sensitive and gifted people have the capacity to sense or see the human energy field, which exists around each of our bodies.

I met these practitioners and clairvoyants while doing my own research with Aura Imaging and Inneractive. In the beginning I was initially skeptical of their claims because I knew there was no proven basis or scientific knowledge about the existence of a human energy field or life energy itself. On the other hand, I knew from my own personal experience that every religion or spiritual group throughout the world was engaged in discussion concerning the essence of human life, human life energy, Chi, Ki or light.

I had the opportunity to perform tests with many of these talented people. Due to my initial skepticism I was somewhat surprised to discover that their claims and abilities were completely verifiable.

The basic purpose of our extensive research was to find and/or establish a relationship between certain personality traits, or human characteristics, with certain color qualities, which are reflected in the human energy field.

Clairvoyants and Vibrational Healing practitioners have mentioned time after time that every living human being radiates an energy field, which is seen as vibrating colors around themselves. Further, that these colors are influenced and change according to the individuals present physical, emotional, mental and spiritual conditions.

This information corresponds closely to Color Psychology, which also works upon the premise that colors and human psychology are closely connected.

Barbara Brennan, one of the world's most acclaimed and gifted healers and teachers, describes in her book, "Hands of Light", explicit details of her countless experiences with seeing the human energy field. Her explorations and extensive research shows that not only personality traits but even the process of sickness and healing is closely connected and reflected within the human energy field.

Pamala Oslie, a clairvoyant counselor from California, describes her experiences as follows: "I developed my ability to see aura colors around humans through my psychic work and through several, intensive training's in which I have actively participated.

Now that I am able to perceive this human energy field it is possible for me to connect the different human aura colors with certain personality traits or behavioral patterns. I use this information productively to create a greater understanding of my clients potential and to help them live a more successful, happy and creative life."

COMMUNICATION AND INTERACTION

Did you know that only 15-30% of our communication is verbal? You might think this is impossible, but it's true. More then 70% of our communication and interaction with our environment are unconscious and nonverbal. Body language, pitch and sound of your voice seem to make up the other 70%. There are those who believe that what we say is not nearly as important as how we say it.

I have found, from my own experience, that the above statement is factual. Sometimes, while trying to explain certain ideas, I seem to invoke and activate feelings and thoughts in my listeners, which I never expected. What I actually said was sometimes completely opposite to what they perceived. I began to wonder, what is the underlying factor in our communication and interaction with other people.

Naturally the tone, pitch and speed of our voice and our body language are important factors in non-verbal communication. But what happens, if you meet someone new, you don't speak with one another at all, and you still perceive certain impressions or feelings about that person? Why is it that even if you are aware of a person's body language, etc., you still get a different impression from them?

Have you ever met someone for the first time and without speaking or communicating in any way you know exactly what type of personality they are? You had an inner feeling, which is often difficult to describe or to formulate. Still, it was clear to you whom you were confronted with.

As I continued my research I probed deeper and deeper, trying to discover what truly determines human interaction. When we come to the understanding that we are all living in a vast ocean of energy and that everything alive is energy; we will move closer to a solution. From an energetic point of view, people are complex systems of life energy, which is manifested, in a certain physical form. Interaction may be defined as one energy system interacting with another energy system.

AURA MASTERY 5:

Stand approximately six feet away from a friend or partner. You can do this exercise with your eyes open or closed. Try to be open and receptive toward the other person. Begin to walk toward your partner and watch your physical, emotional or mental reaction as you come closer. At a certain distance you might begin to feel "different." It might feel as if you have come into their personal environment, their field, or their space.

Does it feel more personal or intimate if you are five feet away or just one foot away? You will probably notice that the closer you are the more personal and intimate it will feel. You will also discover that the results vary with each individual. Some people have a wide personal field, sometimes as much as two to three feet. Others don't seem to be worried or feel threatened, even if you come very close.

If you want to go one step further tune into your partners personal energy field. Feel or sense what kind of person he is? What does he feel right now or what kinds of thoughts are going through his mind? In the beginning it might be difficult to verbalize what you feel but after some practice you will be able to distinguish between the many expressions of energy.

How can this feeling be possible? If we consist only of a solid physical body, we are not supposed to feel or perceive any changes until we actually touch the physical body. But as you have undoubtedly experienced many times, there is in fact a strong interaction and energetic communication occurring.

The human life energy field surrounds our physical body and functions as a buffer, as a field of interaction with our environment. If you are interested in communication and interaction with other people, you should begin to research the concept of human energy fields. Communication is primarily a process and an exchange of information and energy.

THE SPIRAL OF LIFE

Our level of light or life energy determines our direction of growth. We can move *downward* toward entropy, which means decay, aging, a hard life, problems, unconsciousness and darkness. Or we can move *upward* in our spiral of life toward centropy, which means personal and spiritual growth, consciousness, light, fulfillment and connectedness with the universal life energy.

It is my belief and absolute inner knowledge that every human being has to make a conscious decision. The question, which must be asked, is: What direction do I want to take with my life? Do I connect with the upward or the downward spiral. Do I decide to connect with inner healing, peace, personal, spiritual growth and live with the bright light of awareness or do I live an unconscious life filled with resistance and darkness.

There is no real escape for anyone. Negating this decision means putting your head into the sand. Every human being and humanity itself must decide its course of evolution and future development. From a universal point of view this decision must be made.

Do we want to raise our energy and our consciousness to the point of being able to help the planet and ourselves in this time of transition and change, or do we stay unconscious and blindly believe nothing is wrong. We are facing dramatic changes in all areas of life. If we connect with the upward spiral, the high energy or light flow, we will receive all the support we need. To go Inneractive and practice AURA MASTERY means spiraling upward and inward toward healing, harmony and growth.

As our life energy level grows higher, more light will flow in and through us. And, the more we are connected with our life purpose, the more "coincidences" that teach and guide us will happen. We will be more alive and learn to act rather then react. We will receive all the support we need and in this process we will be transformed and move into a higher dimension and therefore reality of human life.

Every human being must now decide which energy spiral they wish to connect with: Either the spiral downward toward lower energy, resistance to growth, a difficult and hard life and unconsciousness, or, the spiral upward and inward to raising your vibration to a higher dimension, connecting to your universal life energy flow, connecting to your inner guidance and a life of prosperity and fulfillment. The spiral upward means a wholistic, fulfilled life, connecting the physical reality with spiritual reality.

AURA MASTERY 6:

It is very easy to tune into the spiral of evolution and spiritual growth. Once you have decided to do this exercise, sit in an upright position with your spine straight. Relax your emotions and your thoughts. Let go of all troubles and feel your physical and your energy body.

Focus your attention at the end of your spine, the mystical place and home of your creative energy. Feel your feet grounded and connected with the earth energy. Visualize a spiral of light developing and imagine this spiral to vibrate in the area of your base chakra. Breathe into the spiral and allow it to expand and grow. You might feel or see a small or a very big energy movement. Continue with whatever works for you.

Feel this spiral get bigger and vibrate faster. Slowly it expands and transcends upwards along your spine. Your body might even move a little bit with this cyclic movement of energy.

Feel this spiral of energy come up your spine where it leaves through the top of your head into eternity. Energy is transformed into a higher state of vibration.

Make sure you always feel grounded with both feet on the ground. Go through several cycles of energy transformation and experience this uplifting feeling of your aura-in-motion.

LIFE ENERGY AND REALITY

Our Aura determines what reality we perceive and experience. If we wish to change our reality and our life, we can use our own life energy-aura to make these changes. The Life Energy Colors reflect our inner reality. They show how we experience life at any given time. These inner vibrations are the key to understanding ourselves and the very meaning of life itself.

Changing our inner reality will create changes in our outer "real" life. Therefore the first step is to have an open mind and the willingness to change your life toward success, prosperity, creativity, happiness and spiritual fulfillment.

We all live in one world, yet experience different realities. We all live on the same planet, but the way we experience our lives might be totally different. Reality is a subjective expression. We tend to view reality as something solid, fixed, something, which cannot be changed. However, if this were true, you would not have the ability to change your reality or change your life in any direction whatsoever.

Why are some people so successful while others are not? How is it possible that you can experience life so totally different from your friends or neighbors? How can it be that many different realities exist within the same space? A beggar can live within the same space as someone who is remarkably wealthy. A caring, loving person can live within the same space as a rude, insensitive person. Space-age technology and stone-age thinking exist together on the same planet.

If you work with AURA MASTERY and start raising your vibration, creating a higher state of awareness you will find the answers within yourself.

ENERGY FOLLOWS THOUGHT

"What you put out, you will get back. As ye sew, so shall ye reap. We become what we think about." The preceding statements echo one universal truth: "Energy follows thought."

There are many different expressions, regardless of religion or philosophy, which clearly show us the same phenomena. Whatever we put out, whatever we decide to do or believe, will ultimately shape and create our own reality.

Anthony Robbins, one of the leading and most respected motivational speakers and teachers of our time, describes three primary decisions, which will shape your life and control your destiny. These decisions are:

1. What you focus on.
2. What things mean to you.
3. What you do to create results.

It is in your hands to create the life you want. You must clearly decide what you want to focus your attention on. You must also decide how you value things, what they really mean to you. Further, and perhaps most important of all, you must decide what actions you are willing to take in order to create the desired results.

The most important aspect in taking control of your own destiny and making changes in your life is to understand and learn how to focus yourself. Many people continue to think the process of focusing means sitting in their living room, concentrating and focusing their mind for countless hours per day, on a certain subject, plan or idea. The more they think about it, the easier it will happen.

Several years ago the Positive Thinking Movement tried to convince people that if they thought only positive thoughts their lives would change. If they would think about success, success would occur. If this were true, everyone would be successful and would live exactly the life they think about.

As I'm sure you are aware, this is not the way it works. Obviously our thoughts are an important part of the process of focusing our attention or energy into a new direction. However, without *e-motion = "energy in motion"*, our thoughts will not have much effect.

Without e-motions our thoughts are as barren as an empty glass. But if you take the time and make the effort to fill the glass with water, you are in charge of the water and as such can do whatever you wish.

Thought requires energy to create real results in real life. Mind plus e-motion creates focus. Energy follows thought.

Awareness - Consciousness - Thought

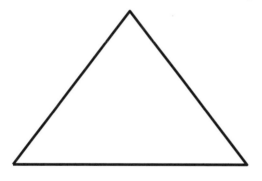

Energy - Emotion   *Reality - Physical result*

Whenever you focus your thinking in a certain direction and integrate or unite it with energy - e-motion - you are the creator of your own life.

Actually, better words for thought would be consciousness or awareness, because thought is a willful effort, which must be made. However, if you are aware or conscious you don't need to do anything. It is much like an inner, passive concentration. But for the ease of our exploration, we will use the word thought.

Let us summarize what we know so far. Our thoughts combined with our energy-in-motion direct our experience and our reality. Our thoughts and our e-motions are reflected in our life energy.

The vibration or quality of life energy is reflected in the colors of the rainbow. With Inneractive AURA VIDEO STATION technology we measure and display your energy and therefore your mind/body connection.

Our life energy colors reflect how we perceive and live our life and what reality we are experiencing at any given time. It also shows how we process life physically, emotionally, mentally and spiritually. Understanding our Life Energy Colors is the first step in creating a healing experience, taking control of our life and shaping our destiny.

Inneractive AURA MASTERY teaches you how to find your own personal tools and instruments for life, achieve concrete results and make changes in your life. After you have started your Inneractive exploration you will practice your knowledge and apply it in your daily life.

INNERACTIVE TECHNOLOGY

It is now time to look into the history of Inneractive technology and AURA MASTERY and how it was developed. Inneractive is a completely new and unique mixture of known, established and fully researched scientific and psychological fields.

Inneractive integrates many different areas including color psychology, mind/body medicine, vibrational therapies, biofeedback, and many other research projects, which have taken place over the last few decades.

One of the corner stones of AURA MASTERY is the Inneractive AURA VIDEO STATION technology, which integrates Biofeedback, Color Psychology and Energy Photography. Inneractive technology provides us with a visual display to measure your Inner World of Mind, Body and Energy in real-time.

To give you a better understanding of how Inneractive technology works, I'd like to look at some areas separately.

BIOFEEDBACK

Biofeedback is the science of measuring and displaying unconscious body functions and then bringing them into consciousness through sound, light and color or other methods of display. Biofeedback is connected with human psycho-physiological behavior (mind-body connection). In general, a measured bio-electric signal is amplified and the information concerning the change is fed back to the subject in a form by which the subject is able to monitor the change and in this fashion learns to control the function.

Biofeedback has actually been used for thousands of years, in many different areas, and known by several different names.

One of the simplest and most basic methods of using biofeedback is to observe your breathing. If we become excited, nervous or stressed, our breathing will become more shallow and quicker than if we remain relaxed and balanced. Therefore, our breathing patterns can offer us helpful information about inner states.

Various other techniques have been used for centuries to provide feedback and energize people's bodies and achieve relaxation and a deep, inner sense of peace and fulfillment. Natural health practitioners and doctors are able to use the pulse as a biofeedback method to find out about conditions of certain organs in our body. In our western culture, Ayurveda is widely known to use the pulse diagnosis as part of its procedures.

The very concept of biofeedback, from a scientific or medical standpoint, needs to be explained more precisely. Clinical Biofeedback does not observe the general body functions, but mainly physiological processes or functions, which are not easily perceived through the human senses.

The measurement of body temperature is a good example for a biofeedback system. We do not possess the senses or organs to immediately perceive our own body temperature. However, if we connect a temperature sensor to our skin and the measured temperature is displayed, we will be able to perceive this information consciously and therefore change it if we wish.

Biofeedback recognizes and interprets measured information and also attempts to influence and change bodily functions and patterns. A typical biofeedback temperature device is a sensor, which is connected to one of your fingers. The measured temperature is then converted and displayed in a digital format.

The biological information is first measured and then fed back to you. After you receive the data through your various senses you have the opportunity to consciously change it.

Another well-known biofeedback system is the one, which measures your brain waves. An electrode, or series of electrodes, is connected to your forehead, where the electricity from your brain is measured. Brain wave activity is then optically displayed on a screen.

Brain waves	Frequency (hertz)	physical condition mental state
Delta	0,2-3,5	sleep, dream state, trance, deep meditation
Theta	3,5-7,5	hypnosis, creativity, mental openness
Alpha	7,5-13	silence, relaxed condition, quiet thought
Beta	13-	daily activity, outward directed awareness

Naturally, and understandably, there are many other biofeedback methods. The main point you should be aware of is that biofeedback is used throughout the world with many different applications. Biofeedback can display and introduce you to functions and areas within yourself, which you may not have been aware of. Biofeedback is a tool to help you understand the shadow-unconscious parts within yourself and to bring them into light-consciousness.

COLOR PSYCHOLOGY

Since the beginning of time color has played a significant role in every day life in virtually every society known to mankind. Chiefs, warriors and medicine men from various tribes dramatically used colors to frighten their opponents or to show certain positions in their society. Colors produce and revealed by nature and in particular, sunlight, were used in everyday life.

Over the last three centuries, scientists, healers and psychologists have become aware of the importance of colors and started to research their significance into more and more detail.

Throughout recorded history many attempts have been made to classify or integrate the different human personality characters, the nature of man and its connection with colors, into systems, which we are able to learn from and understand. These classifications focus on inner processes and give us in depth information about a person's inner life.

Hippocrates developed one of the very first personality systems in ancient Greece. His model, which he referred to as, the "Four Temperaments", divided human personalities into four major and completely distinctive groups. For informational purposes, Hippocrates named his "Four Temperaments" sanguine, phlegmatic, melancholic and choleric.

Over the last three hundred years, scientists, healers and psychologists have become acutely aware of the importance of colors and their connection with human emotional or mental conditions.

The famous physician Paracelsus, regarded as one of the founders of wholistic and natural medicine, was aware of the importance of colors and personality traits. He used that knowledge in many of his treatments. The yellow warmth of the sun was used in various treatments as was the orange qualities of sunrise.

In the 18th century the German poet Johann Wolfgang von Goethe felt his research and writings on colors were the most important of his contributions. His work, "The Theory of Colors", is still considered as a masterwork on colors and their effect on human behavior. Goethe was convinced that colors have a strong effect on the human body and psyche. He believed strongly in the close connection between colors and feelings.

During the last few decades the field of psychology has also recognized there are basically only a few, typical, human behavioral patterns or personality types. Carl G. Jung, the founder of modern psychology, has used the term "archetypes" to describe the deep-rooted structures of human behavior. In the early 1920's Jung developed his now considered classical, "Theory of personality types".

Since 1970 worldwide recognition has been granted to Max Luescher, the noted Swiss psychologist. His "Luescher Color Test" is used internationally by other well-known psychologists, counselors and healing professionals. His work laid the foundation for the acceptance and the importance of colors, especially when used in the healing professions.

For the first time since psychology was accepted as a science, the Luescher Color Test found a direct connection between different archetypes, respective psychological patterns and the qualities of colors. The Luescher test has been used successfully for more than 40 years by health professionals and in all facets of business counseling.

However, the Luescher test focuses primarily on the psychological aspects of our personality and uses only a partial wholistic approach.

Color therapy offers additional information about the connection of color qualities with certain personality traits and even physical function in various areas of the body. In color therapy certain colors are used to both influence and treat emotional, psychological and physical problems.

For example, Red indicates a stimulation of our physical body and our nervous system. Green is stabilizing and balances. Blue calms our emotions and thoughts and creates peace and expansion.

With color therapy we find a clear connection and interaction between the effects of colors and psycho-emotional states.

VIBRATIONAL THERAPIES AND MINDBODY MEDICINE

Over the last few decades vibrational or energy medicine and mind/body knowledge has grown tremendously. Treating only the physical body, without looking at the deeper cause of the problem from a wholistic point of view, is like fixing the empty gas gauge in your car if your tank is empty.

Since the pioneering research of Psycho-Neuroimmunology, the study of the links between thoughts and emotions, the brain, the nervous system and the immune system - science and medicine has been exploring the influence of our mind and our health. Our mind is interconnected with the physical body and visa versa. It should be our goal to explore this connection even further to the point where both science and we as individuals understand it and are able to use it in our everyday life.

Vibrational medicine refers to the electro-magnetic nature of men. Sub-atomic physics has demonstrated that everything which exists, even matter, is nothing more than units of energy in empty space. Electrons are orbiting around the nucleus within an atom the same as planets orbit around the sun. We are beings of energy in different forms and densities.

Eastern medicine has been using this knowledge for many centuries. Acupuncture, Ayurveda and homeopathy are just a few of these well-know methods of treatments being used today. Vibrational therapies, or medicine, which is an overall term for techniques and treatments based on the energetic nature of man, is actually a new scientific field and will be the subject of many research projects over the next years.

"Mind/body connection" has virtually become a household name in the 90's. Nearly everyone has heard of it and many people are beginning to look deeper into their own mind/body connection.

Mind/body medicine, or therapies, basically uses a wholistic approach to treat and heal. But mind/body knowledge should not only be used for medical treatments. For me, it is more a way of life. If we understand our Inneractive connection we will connect with the flow of life.

REAL LIFE EXAMPLES

Before I go into various applications, I'd like to share with you an up close and personal example of how AURA MASTERY can make significant changes in our lives. This one story is especially wonderful.

A married couple, John and Christine, decided to use Inneractive AURA MASTERY at home to both explore themselves and get along better. For the last few months their relationship had been plagued with fights, arguments and confrontations. Their problems also extended into their professional life. John was not very satisfied with his job. He was on the verge of being laid off and as a result was not in a very positive state.

Both of them knew they had to do something. After they sat down in front of the AURA VIDEO STATION they were not surprised. When John's aura scan came up on the screen he slowly shook his head and said, "Amazing. The colors really relate to what I'm feeling inside. I just didn't want to accept it!" His aura colors were Dark Red and Orange and there was very little movement in his energy field.

John's Dark Red and Orange indicated he was in a state of survival, over activity and excitement. He was trying to get all of his energy from the outside world. It was increasingly difficult for him to relax and to recharge his life energy batteries. John was basically fighting for energy to survive in his personal as well as his professional life.

Christine, on the other hand, was not surprised to see a light Blue in her own Aura. She was in a totally different state of energy than John. Her Blue energy field indicated a sensitive state with deep feelings and a tendency to avoid problems.

At the time, she was not aware that her first reaction in most cases was to try and create peace and harmony, even if it was virtually impossible. Christine would willingly give her energy to anyone in order to avoid problems or altercations.

John and Christine began to understand their pattern. John would express his passionate and powerful Red feelings and Christine would react to his assertiveness with weak and sensitive introversion. This energetic reaction is certain to create situations, which are out of harmony.

John started to learn to change his energy. After practicing several weeks AURA MASTERY he found it much easier to achieve a relaxed Green or Blue State of energy. Being able to actually see the constant feedback through the Aura Video Station allowed him to master his energy to the point where he could sit quietly relax, and raise his own energy level.

Through AURA MASTERY, Christine learned how to better protect herself and not give away all of her energy. She also learned how to express her feelings and her power without the fear of being rejected.

As a result of this process, John was able to connect with his creative potential. Because he was now able to relax and let go, his life energy balanced in a bright and light Orange color. He suddenly felt great energy from within. He was as powerful and strong as ever. He changed his focus from survival and fear into creativity and success. New business opportunities surfaced and he began to be extremely successful.

Christine continued teaching school. She was impressed by her own strength and power after practicing the AURA MASTERY. She started to speak her own truth, even when confronted with problems. She also felt a new depth in her openness and love for children and people in general. Christine stabilized in a radiating, Green-Blue life energy color showing her heartful and nurturing personality.

Magically, John's and Christine's personal life began to improve. By understanding their energetic patterns and by mastering their life energy they started to find new levels of harmony in their relationship. It also shows that healing happens once we understand our state of mind, body and energy and make changes accordingly.

My own story is another example of success with AURA MASTERY. After more then eight years of practicing meditation, breathing, and yoga techniques, I did not consider myself as a newcomer or beginner. I feel a true connection with my Self and a strong sensitivity for my physical body. In my meditations or after creating a high-energy state, I am able to see and perceive my energy field. But the Inneractive Aura Video Station opened another dimension in my life.

Using the Inneractive Aura Video Station technology made me acutely aware that my emotions are much more powerful then I ever thought they could be. It not only revealed my emotional reactions, but also showed emotional reactions, which I didn't know, even existed.

A typical reaction in my life was to repress and block feelings of anger or aggression. I would just pretend everything was fine. But later I would experience tension in my lower back or feel overly excited. Perhaps this sounds familiar to you. The Aura Video Station reflected these unconscious reactions before they showed up in my physical body and created problems or disharmony.

Let me offer a typical example: I was asked about, or would be thinking about a certain person, and almost instantaneously my Aura would reveal a strong reaction, namely a repression of energy.

At the beginning of my AURA MASTERY practice I was not aware of these energetic reactions at all. But after several similar reactions I began to understand what was happening. It felt as if this energy was coming into light from deep within, being clearly revealed and fed back to me in order to regain my power and responsibility.

I have seen many more examples from my own experience or from many other practitioners and users around the world. AURA MASTERY will be a powerful tool for you. The only obstacle you have to overcome is to start practicing and using it.

AURA MASTERY

The first part of the AURA MASTERY process consists of different levels of activity and participation:

♦ **AURA COLOR TEST**

♦ **AURA VIDEO STATION live aurafeedback**

♦ **AURA MASTERY PRACTICE**

The first 3 steps of AURA MASTERY are to go through the AURA COLOR TEST, to practice all AURA MASTERY EXERCISES and at the same time to work with the AURA VIDEO STATION and it's live aurafeedback system.

The **AURA COLOR TEST** will help you to find your Color Personality Type and to discover the real meaning of colors and their relationships with certain personality traits, mind/body behavior, etc.

The Inneractive **AURA VIDEO STATION** will give you a true and real-time feedback of your State of Mind, Body and Energy. To see your colorful aura on a computer or television screen is not only exciting but also very therapeutic and educational. It can help you in your journey towards balance, well being and individual growth.

Each **AURA MASTERY EXERCISE** will teach you how to get in touch with your Aura and your emotional-energetic nature. It will help you to increase your energy level and to raise your vibration to a higher level of awareness. The AURA MASTERY TEST will help you find your "low energies and vibes" in your life and it will make sure you start your daily practice of "increasing your energy and raising your vibration".

Now, let's go to the first part – the AURA COLOR TEST.

AURA COLOR TEST

The *Inneractive Aura Color Test* is your first step of your journey toward self-discovery and healing.

I believe it is essential to all of us to know and understand our personality type. If we know our mind/body reactions, our beliefs and motivations, our social and interpersonal behavior, our goals and desires, and also know who we are and how we function, we can go beyond our personality becoming a multi-dimensional person radiating all the colors of the rainbow. We are no longer limited to one color of the rainbow. Rather, we have the freedom to live whatever color quality we want.

From my own as well as thousands of other people's experiences, I know that the Inneractive Aura Color Test can help you to:

- Understand yourself better.
- Know your deep routed mind/body interactions and behavioral patterns
- Create more fulfilling relationships with yourself, your partner, friends and family.
- Understand other people better, which is helpful not only in personal relationships, but also in business, negotiations, communication, etc.
- Create acceptance and understanding between people that at times can seem to be extremely different.
- Find your strong qualities and let go of weak, adapted, unnecessary personality traits and behavior.
- Find answers to many questions about yourself
- Connect with your Self, which goes far beyond personality.

Therefore, I invite you to find and explore your Inneractive Aura Color Personality Type.

AURA COLOR TEST INTRODUCTION

Over the past years, several different color personality tests have been used. One of the potential downfalls with color tests is that you have to choose your own colors or color combinations. And, your choice of these colors provides the basis and the premise for the profile test or the psychological study.

Choosing colors is a very subjective process. It can be influenced by culture, race or even religious beliefs and may not accurately reflect the true personality or psyche of a person. These choices may even be influenced by the client's current taste in fashion. The process is subjective and as a result can sometimes be inaccurate.

There is a second reason why most ordinary color tests only work in a limited fashion. We as human beings have the capacity to be extremely clever. We are continually finding reasons to either do things or not to do things. It is not uncommon for people to look for the easy way to do things and on occasion to even alter the truth if it proves to be more favorable to us.

Over the years I've had the opportunity to observe many people consciously pick certain colors in a standard color test simply because they knew some basics about the colors themselves. I know with a certainty that some participants would pick Violet or White because they are supposedly considered to be more spiritual. Others would choose the color Blue because it represents peacefulness and calmness.

With the Inneractive AURA VIDEO STATION we have eliminated the issue of "subjective" color choices. We will connect you with special developed Bio Sensor, which actually measure your own energy activity and state of mind and body within you.

Even, if a questionnaire is included in this book I recommend using an Inneractive AURA VIDEO STATION to find your Aura Color Type.

The Inneractive AURA VIDEO STATION technology and AURA MASTERY were developed over years of research with tens of thousands of people being tested with Biofeedback Imaging Systems. We have also incorporated and assimilated vast research, which has been accumulated by other experts in the field of Biofeedback, Life Energy and Color Psychology.

Once you have found your own Aura Color Personality Type either through the AURA COLOR TEST questionnaire or through the LIVE AURA VIDEO STATION, read the explanations describing the personality of this particular aura color.

Each Aura Color Personality is divided into five different sections. These sections will give you insight into how you process reality and what tools, instruments, strong and weak points you experience in life.

The sections are:

MIND/BODY

How do you express yourself, how do you process feelings and emotions? How can you express and transform your emotions into creativity? How do you think, how can you expand your mental abilities and use them for your best interest? What exercises or sports are good for you? What do you believe in, what meaning has spirituality or religion to you? What are your mission, vision and your life purpose? What is your motivation for doing things?

SOCIAL LIFE

What social position are you comfortable with, how do you interact with society, how do you communicate with yourself and others?

RELATIONSHIPS AND INTIMACY

What types of relationships are good for you, who are you compatible with, what type of partner do you attract, how do you experience sex and intimacy?

CAREER AND FINANCES

What jobs and occupations are suitable for you? What does career mean to you? What is your leadership style and how do you interact with others in your business environment? How do you handle finances and what is your connection to money? How do you react when confronted with problems and what is your best way of solving your own and other people's problems?

HEALTH, WELL-BEING AND GROWTH

How can you recharge your life energy batteries, what tools can you use to achieve well-being, harmony and personal power, what will help you in your personal growth, how can you live your full potential, how do you achieve Mind/Body harmony and personal and spiritual growth?

TEST INSTRUCTIONS

There are several different options as to how you can use the Aura Color Test. If you wish to expand your knowledge about the different personality types you should read all 12 Personality Modes. If you wish to find your own Personality Mode simply connect yourself with your Aura-in-motion System or an AURA VIDEO STATION™ to measure and display your Aura Colors. If you don't have an Inneractive Aura System available, you can go through the following questionnaire to find your Aura Color Personality Type.

First, go through all statements in each area to find your own Personality Mode. The more you can identify with a question or statement, the more likely you are to be this personality type. If you read a statement and think, *"Yes, that's me"* or, *"Yes, sometimes, maybe"*, check this statement. After you have gone through all Personality Types, simply add up where you have made the most 'Yes' answers.

As an example: If you have checked 5 Reds, 9 Oranges, 4 Yellows, etc., you would obviously go to the Orange Personality chapter and explore it further.

As you go through the questionnaire, responding to the statements, stay open and look into yourself. Be as honest and as truthful as you can. Don't hide anything or try to manufacture feelings or thoughts. By being deceitful the only person you deceive is yourself.

Second, try to distinguish between your own personality traits and attitudes or behavior, which have been adopted or accumulated. Often, over a period of years, we take on other peoples personality traits without even noticing. Our parents, partners or social and business environment often have a strong impact on us. Your key goal is to find your own Personality Mode, not that of your parents, friends or associates. Keeping this uppermost in your mind will help you in distinguishing and answering the statements with an inner clarity.

Thirdly, you might find yourself represented in more than one Personality Mode. Our experience is that many people will very clearly connect with one personality type. Others will find several modes as their own. Therefore, don't hesitate to go through several Personality Modes. If you agree with more then 6 statements in any Personality Mode you should explore it further.

Always remember that we are rainbows and not just one color. We have the capacity to expand ourselves and live out all the color qualities we need or desire. But before we can do that, we need to understand our Inner World and we also should know our deep routed personality traits, behaviors, beliefs and motivations.

The Aura Color Test is a starting point for the journey into yourself. If you wish to explore a more sophisticated selection process use the *Inneractive* **MULTIMEDIA AURA COLOR TEST** program. It features an Interactive Questionnaire, audio and multimedia design, and the Book of Wisdom where you can find your personal Keys of Wisdom.

QUESTIONNAIRE

Use the questionnaire or statements for each color personality to find your own Personality Mode. Remember, this is not a test rather an exploration into your personality, your mind/body and your behavioral patterns.

The following summary will guide you through the process:

1. Go through all 12 Color Personality statements and check the statements, which you feel reflect yourself.

2. Find the Personality Mode with the most 'Yes, that's me - sometimes' statements.

3. Go to the Color Personality Summary and verify your choice before you continue.

4. Once you have determined which Personality Mode you want to explore further, go to the corresponding chapter.

5. Read your Personality Mode and try to use the information given in your daily life.

6. Come back to the questionnaire to explore other Personality Modes.

7. Ask your partner, friends and family to find their Aura Color Personality Type.

DEEP - RED - WORKER

___ I am a realist and believe only in what I can see and touch.

___ I am loyal and supportive to my family, community or society.

___ I don't talk a lot about my inner thoughts and feelings.

___ Sometimes I have an explosive temper and I react physically.

___ I have a strong physical constitution, slow body movements.

___ Hanging out in bars with friends is more fun then staying home.

___ I love to watch sports, like football, boxing, and soccer.

___ I am sexual and I love to express my animalistic feelings.

___ Regularly I have to deal with survival, fights, confrontations.

___ Practical and hardheaded would best describe me.

___ I need to achieve immediate, tangible and concrete results.

___ Stamina, strength and teamwork are my strong points.

_____

___ Total 'Yes' statements

RED - WINNER

___ I express myself through my physical body and my sexuality.

___ I love the excitement of a fast, desireful, stimulating life.

___ I am competitive, successful and need to achieve results.

___ I tend to be honest, blunt, straightforward and very direct.

___ I am powerful, self-confident, independent and practical.

___ I can have a very eccentric, individual and unique behavior.

___ I am impulsive, stimulating and explosive in my interactions.

___ Passionate, sexual relationships or affairs are very important.

___ Sex is a desire filled, sensual and exciting experience.

___ I need freedom and independence in my relationships.

___ I am a winner and leader. I can achieve whatever I want.

___ I need to be the center of attention.

_____ Total 'Yes' statements

ORANGE   -   ADVENTURER

___ I love the excitement of shaping and forming physical reality.

___ I enjoy all the pleasures and adventures life has to offer.

___ I always imagine and plan strategies for my next project.

___ I think and plan very precisely, detailed, step-by-step.

___ Letting go, passivity and relaxation are not my priorities.

___ I appear to be powerful, strong, forceful and sometimes pushy.

___ I need to be in control of my life, my relationships, my career.

___ I am not interested what other people think or feel about me.

___ My freedom and independence are most important to me.

___ I am interested in projects, business, sales or marketing.

___ I talk mainly about my projects and challenges.

___ Sex is fun and pleasure, a great adventure.

___

___ Total 'Yes' statements

YELLOW-BROWN   -   SCIENTIST

___ I love to create, shape and form ideas and concepts.

___ I am a very logical, analytical, rational and sequential thinker.

___ I prefer to see the proof, logic and data behind reality.

___ I need order, stability, structure and security.

___ I love to study, learn or discuss my ideas and concepts.

___ I like to have regular routines in my day-to-day life.

___ I talk very slowly and detailed. I think first, then I talk.

___ A safe home and a stable family are important to me.

___ I prefer solid, long-lasting and committed relationships.

___ I enjoy working with mechanical or electronic gadgets.

___ I prefer a secure, stable work with regular income.

___ I am honest, reliable and trustworthy. People count on me.

_____ Total 'Yes' statements

YELLOW - ENTERTAINER

___ I need to have fun, play, exercise or be around people.

___ I am happy, sunny, joyful, easy-going and enjoy life.

___ I need body movement, exercise, dancing on a regular basis.

___ My body is very sensitive and acts like a biological antenna.

___ I can be very spontaneous, overflowing with creative ideas.

___ I am a very bright, intelligent and radiant individual.

___ I love to travel, relax on a beach or dance all night long.

___ I look younger then my real age.

___ I don't want responsibilities or commitments.

___ I like to be artistic, creative or work with my hands.

___ I am good in starting new projects, but bad in finishing them.

___ I am always late for my meetings.

____ Total 'Yes' statements

GREEN   -   TEACHER

___ I am very social, communicative and natural.

___ Nature and people are very important to me.

___ I love animals especially dogs, horses and cats.

___ I like to teach, communicate or give other people advice.

___ I talk for hours about many different subjects.

___ I need peace, harmony and balance in my life.

___ I love to be with my close friends, relatives and family.

___ I am open, quick-minded and communicative.

___ Relationships and friends are most important in my life.

___ Intimacy means love, affection and sharing.

___ Others consider me as a good teacher, therapist, counselor.

___ I need to share and express my inner feelings.

_____

____ Total 'Yes' statements

DEEP-GREEN - ORGANIZER

___ I love to learn and to be intellectually stimulated all the time.

___ I am quick-minded with a precise and accurate memory.

___ I am ambitious, competitive, goal-oriented and expect the best.

___ I have a strong personality, perseverance and self-esteem.

___ Wealth, luxury and money represent social status and power.

___ I articulate and communicate very quickly, clearly and directly.

___ I am conservative in my beliefs and behavior.

___ I am attractive and wear only expensive or exclusive clothing.

___ I have high expectations in my partner, friends and jobs.

___ I am a workaholic and perfectionist in working on my career.

___ I prefer independent, high level or well-paid executive jobs.

___ I rather develop plans and ideas than do the actual work.

_____ Total 'Yes' statements

BLUE - HELPER

____ I am very peaceful, caring and supportive.

____ I am more concerned about others than about myself.

____ Love, God and spirituality are important to me.

____ I want to be loved and appreciated.

____ I have a slow metabolism with cold hand and feet.

____ I am very social and I love to be around people all the time.

____ I am conservative and family oriented with strong values.

____ I want a healthy, loving and caring relationship.

____ Love and affection are more important then sex or passion.

____ I have problems setting boundaries or saying no.

____ I am a born caretaker, advisor, counselor or healer.

____ I am not very ambitious or goal-oriented.

____ Total 'Yes' statements

INDIGO - SEEKER

___ Trust, loyalty and honesty are very important.

___ Life is love and compassion.

___ I follow my intuition and my inner guidance.

___ I feel artistic, creative and spiritually advanced.

___ I am soft and sensitive yet aware and independent.

___ I am a clear and intuitive but also conservative thinker.

___ I need a safe and secure environment around me.

___ Spirituality and love are more important then sex and passion.

___ I have difficulty relating to my body or physical reality.

___ I prefer to express myself through music, dance or art.

___ I need the freedom to live my inner beliefs and principals.

___ I love to help and support others in their growth.

___ Total 'Yes' statements

VIOLET - VISIONARY

___ I am a visionary, intuitive and innovative thinker.

___ I feel physical and powerful yet sensitive and intuitive.

___ I want to be famous or do something important in my life.

___ Often I am scattered or involved in too many projects at once.

___ I want to inspire and help improve the planet or humanity.

___ I appear to be magnetic and powerful with a magical aura.

___ I end up in leadership positions or the center of attention.

___ I am very passionate and sensual with a strong sex drive.

___ I love the passion and power of music.

___ Success means to live my vision and fulfill my destiny.

___ Money represents power, influence and possibilities.

___ I need to be independent with the freedom to live my vision.

___ Total 'Yes' statements

LAVENDER - DREAMER

___ My physical body is very fragile and sensitive.

___ I am an imaginative, inspirational and artistic thinker.

___ I believe in dreams, angels, spirits, higher dimensions of life.

___ I don't like to focus and concentrate for long periods of time.

___ I live by my feelings and intuition, not my rational mind.

___ I love to talk about my ideas, fantasies and dreams.

___ I am creative and full of wonder and imagination.

___ I have bad memory, I am often late, suddenly change plans.

___ I love soft, meditative music, candles and incense.

___ I prefer to work in relaxed, low stressed environments.

___ I have problems finishing projects.

___ I prefer artistic, healing or metaphysical activities.

___ Total 'Yes' statements

WHITE - HEALER

_____ I have a transcendent and radiant appearance.

_____ I am very sensitive, vulnerable and easily overwhelmed.

_____ I can tune into other dimensions of existence or reality.

_____ Meditation, spirituality, awareness, healing are priorities.

_____ I need to stay in a healing and transcendent state of mind.

_____ My inner connection with God is most important to me.

_____ I tend to be introverted, withdrawn and quiet.

_____ I am sensitive to other people's emotions and thoughts.

_____ I take on other people's energies and qualities very easily.

_____ I need a lot of time alone to recharge myself.

_____ I choose to work in quiet, calm, peaceful environments.

_____ I love to work with individuals in healing or counseling.

_____ Total 'Yes' statements

AURA COLOR PERSONALITY TYPES

The following list of action words is a summary of the Inneractive Aura Color Personality Types as determined from our worldwide Inneractive research with ten thousands of people.

The AURA COLOR TEST distinguishes between the following 12 different color personalities.

1. **DEEP-RED**   Physical, hardworking, action, power, survival, realistic, physical active, vital force, grounded, strength, stamina, physical explorer.

2. **RED**   Excitement, physical, energetic, competitive, leader, winner, achiever, winner, courage, will power, sexual, entrepreneur, promoter.

3. **ORANGE**   Pleasure, enjoyment, challenge, thrill, positive action oriented, productive, physical and creative expression, adventurer, business.

4. **YELLOW/ BROWN**   Analytical, intellectual, detail oriented, logical, structure, security, scientific, honest, reliable, perfectionist, precise in thoughts and actions.

5. **YELLOW**   Playful, sunny, creative, fun, learning, light movement, entertainer, radiates optimism, warmth, charming, generous, easy going.

6. **GREEN**   Social, nature, content, harmony, teacher, loves to communicate and share with others, most social type, perfect host or hostess.

7. **DEEP-GREEN** Quick minded, goal-oriented, wealth, material, communicative, luxury, leader, responsibility, organizer, driving force, ambitious planer.

8. **BLUE** Caring, sensitive, loving, helpful, loyal, helper, compassion, peaceful, desire to be of service and to help and support others, nurturing.

9. **INDIGO** Clarity, calm, deep inner feelings, love, seeker introverted, inner knowing, authenticity, high, sense of inner values, artistic.

10. **VIOLET** Intuitive, artistic, idealistic, magical, sensual, theorist, futuristic, visionary, charismatic, non-conformist, possibilities, innovative inventors.

11. **LAVENDER** Imagination, mystical, daydreamer, fantasy, artistic, soft, creative, fragile, sensitive, often appear spacy, unrealistic or etheric.

12. **WHITE** Transcendent, transformation, clear, spiritual, healing, quiet, enlightened, sensitive, live in higher dimensions, strong spiritual connection.

DEEP-RED PERSONALITIES

The following are the qualities and action words associated with DEEP-RED personalities:

Area	Description
Physical	Hardworking, physical, realistic, grounded, practical, expression of vital force, overworked, stressed.
Emotional	Intensely physical, emotional energy, often unexpressed, loyal, strength, trustworthy, perseverant, honest, but also anger, rage.
Mental	Linear, realistic, physical orientation, will power, forceful, thinking.
Spiritual	Physical ideals, God is physical entity, not an important concept.
Motivation	Survival, physical expression, physical appetite and exploration.
Mission/ Vision	Explore physical reality without fear, find creative expressions.
Growth	Slow, but sometimes explosive, linear, simple.
Exercise	Powerful, physical activities, like boxing, body building, football.
Recharge battery	Harmonious physical and emotional expression, focus on positive beliefs and creative projects, confront their fears and survival feelings.
Communication	Slow but strong, deep voice, simple language.
Interaction	Love to work and physically help others, overpowering, intense.
Relationships	Loners, partner provides basic needs for living, security.
Social, Friends	Conservative, adjust to society, hang out with friends in clubs

Sex, Intimacy	Emotionally open only to close friends, physical pleasure.
Money	Security, survival, often needs to work hard for their money.
Success	Express themselves and explore physical reality, often need to go through hard work, struggles or resistance to achieve results.
Occupation	Enjoy all physical work and activities.
Career	Keep others going, powerful helpers and support people.

MIND/BODY

Deep-Red personalities are physical, grounded and realistic. They live a powerful and intense life, interacting with physical reality, as they know it. They experience life on a physical level and love to explore all possibilities, which the physical world has to offer. They believe mostly in what they can perceive through their five senses. To them life is very simple and very real.

Deep-Red personalities motivation in life is to experience physical reality with courage, strength and fullness. They have to go beyond feelings and thoughts of survival, resistance and fear to live to their full potential. Deep-Reds are powerful individuals who know the importance of physical reality and its wonders.

Deep-Reds normally have strong physical constitutions and love to express themselves through their bodies. They are easily recognized by their well-developed physiques. They also need to express their powerful physical energy to stay balanced and centered. Because of their strong physical appearance and energy, hard physical work and sports are wonderful activities for these strong personalities. Physical movement, either in work or sports, is necessary channels for their forceful, earth-life energy to be expressed and released.

Sports, like bodybuilding, boxing and other activities which need impulsive, powerful, physical energy are good ways of expressing their life energy.

In harmony, Deep-Reds are physically very strong and powerful. Courage, trustworthiness, perseverance and honesty are their strongest attributes. They are hard working personalities with an intensive desire to live and to stay alive. A Deep-Red's life purpose is to explore and experience the physical world with joy, courage and energy. It is necessary for them to confront challenges and to go beyond their fears. Deep-Reds in harmony express themselves physically and emotionally and have a very joyful and positive outlook towards life.

Deep-Red personalities are practical and down-to-earth. They are conservative thinkers and perceive life through their physical, practical mind. Their thinking is not abstract or very complex. Reality is very tangible for them. A fact is fact. They believe only in what they can see, hear, feel and smell.

Abstract or philosophical concepts or thoughts make them emotional or physically uneasy or impatient. They don't have the time or the patience to think about unrealistic ideas. On the other hand, Deep-Reds love to explore physical reality with all its complexities and possibilities.

Philosophies, mental ideas and sensitivity are alien concepts for them. Because Deep-Reds are not very interested in unorthodox or unfamiliar concepts they often blindly accept societies way of living and go along with mass consciousness. They are loyal toward their families, governments and society. Living within the rules of society give Deep-Reds a certain security and a knowledge that they have done things the correct way.

Deep-Reds are sincere and honest. In harmony, they know how to express their intense emotional and physical energies. They have learned to control or direct their powerful force into positive, creative directions.

Deep-Reds are practical, hardheaded and hard working. They love to achieve immediate results. As a result of enjoying such an active, intense physical life, they are usually overworked, overactive and stressed. They have difficulties in relaxing and letting go inside.

Being overworked and overactive is a common situation in an unbalanced Deep-Reds life. They cannot be told to be passive or to relax. Their powerful energy drives them forward and gives them enough stamina and strength to do the work of two people. They will always be physically active and busy. They are constantly on the run, one activity after the other, often having several jobs at the same time.

They try to provide a good physical life for themselves and their family. Their deepest fear is of death and poverty. They are regularly confronted with survival, conflicts and other challenges in their lives. Contrary to most peoples beliefs and the impression they normally give, Deep-Reds are sensitive and easily hurt. However, they have a tendency of not showing their sensitivity. Rather, they cover it up with powerful, strong behavior. Deep-Reds project their anger and frustrations onto others because they are both impulsive and explosive.

Deep Reds express their emotions and feelings very naturally. Much like animals they have a need to eliminate their impulsive, intense, powerful physical and emotional energy. They just tough it out, no matter, who gets hurt. Deep-Reds have to express their feelings through their physical bodies. Quite often, they do not understand this reactive process.

On the other hand, Deep-Reds have problems communicating their innermost feelings. They have to learn to talk about or share their secrets. Being sensitive and clear about their feelings is an essential step towards a free expression of their inner self.

If Deep-Red personalities are out of harmony they will exhibit an impulsive, explosive or violent temper. If things don't go their way they will be annoyed, frustrated, physically explosive or potentially dangerous. Out of power, their rage is often released through their physical bodies.

They unconsciously let go of their intense, "stuck" energy through aggressive actions, such as a physical fight or even destroying and damaging physical property.

Deep-Reds have to understand that they need to express this powerful energy which is inside of them through their physical body. It's not a matter of thinking about it or solving problems emotionally or mentally. They need to find a physical outlet. Once they find positive channels of expression, Deep-Reds will be productive, creative and happy individuals.

Deep-Reds can be stubborn. Once they have decided on a direction, it is difficult for them to stop or even change. They want things their way. Openness for new situations and flexibility are important qualities to understand and learn.

Deep-Reds often experience an emotional overload. They have an abundance of emotional and physical energy, but have difficulties in expressing this powerful force. Emotional outbursts are often the only solution to release the accumulated emotions. If Deep-Reds haven't learned to express their powerful energy or if they are afraid and hold back their power, they will experience unhappiness.

Not expressing and living their emotions is the worst thing that can happen for them. They will feel depressed, powerless, overloaded and find no reasons to live. Unexpressed emotions will accumulate inside and create many problems. Therefore, Deep-Reds need to be sensitive towards their inner feelings and emotions and they need to find positive, creative outlets for their powerful energies.

It is not easy for Deep-Reds to open up toward others. They hide their innermost feelings and thoughts and are often seen as insensitive, loud and brutally intense beings. They need to understand that being sensitive doesn't mean to be childish or soft. Developing physical and emotional sensitivity is an important step toward success.

Spirituality or religion are not important issues in their lives yet they go to church to enjoy the social aspects. Deep-Reds like the meetings and get-togethers during or after church but in reality are not very concerned with religion. Physical reality and nature are reflections of God. They want to understand and experience all that physical reality has to offer.

SOCIAL LIFE

Deep-Reds are conservative thinkers. They have very few problems with living and accepting the rules and norms of society. Actually, it gives them a sense of security and belonging. Deep-Reds are found in all areas of society. They are wonderful helpers and support their families and communities to the best of their abilities.

Deep-Reds love to just hang out with their friends, drink a beer, and watch football, soccer or boxing. This is relaxing for them and they are often seen more in their favorite bar, with friends, then at home. They need other people in their life. Community lets them forget their fear of being alone and not alive.

Verbal communication is not the favorite activity of a Deep-Reds. Most the time they are not very articulate. They prefer simple get-togethers much more than sophisticated, intellectual conversations. Even if Deep-Reds do enjoy parties, they are careful with whom they get involved. They will open up only for their long-time friends or people they know they can trust.

Deep-Reds like people who are on their own level of understanding. Experiencing, sharing and talking about their world of action, sports, achievements and even sex, means fun to them.

RELATIONSHIPS AND INTIMACY

It is a major challenge for a Deep-Red personality to live in a sensitive, long-lasting, emotional and open relationship. Although they love to go out with friends, they rarely open themselves to deeper connections. Deep-Reds enjoy expressing their "animal" desires and their emotional energies, which often is not a good basis for sensitive, intimate relationships. On the other hand, Deep-Reds are very loyal once they have committed to a partner.

In power, Deep-Reds carry no resentments or prejudices toward sexuality or a lustful life. To them, sexuality *is* life and shows them their aliveness. It is a natural expression of love and power. An orgasm is one of the few ways Deep-Reds can reach an ecstatic state of mind. Sex doesn't necessarily involve love and compassion, but is a physical pleasure to be enjoyed and experienced. To express themselves through their physical body, live emotions fully and enjoy sex is a natural state of being.

Deep-Reds are loners. They need a certain amount of time for themselves. Their partners should allow them enough physical freedom and independence to explore their own world at their own pace.

Deep-Reds are usually compatible with Yellow-Brown or other Deep-Red personalities. They feel understood and like each others stability, reliability and their like-minded, physical attitude and behavior. These Color Personalities will mirror their own strong and weak points which often isn't enough to go beyond their known reality and possibilities.

Deep-Reds also like to be around Blue or Green personalities. However, they might not understand their sensitivity, deep feelings and their need to communicate either emotionally or verbally. Even so, they can still learn a lot from each other. Yellows usually have difficulties with a Deep-Reds stability, realism and heaviness.

Deep-Reds seem to have more difficulties in relating with Lavender and White personalities. These personality types are at the opposite end of the color spectrum and therefore experience life completely different. Understanding and sensitivity will help these personality types to get along much better.

Deep-Reds might have problems with a Deep-Greens ambitions and mental power. And it is very likely that Violets or Indigos will be too far out, futuristic or too sensitive for a Deep-Reds realistic perceptions. Therefore they might stay away from each other.

Deep-Red personalities usually get along with most other personality types as along as they can have enough physical space for themselves. Their biggest challenge is to not only create convenient relationships on a physical level, but real, intimate relationships on a emotional, mental and spiritual level.

CAREER AND FINANCES

Deep-Reds prefer physical work to almost anything else. These hard working personalities integrate perseverance and stamina. They shine whenever strong physical power and strength are needed. They are excellent in finishing projects because they have the stamina and are willing to push themselves over limits where many other color personalities aren't willing to go.

Deep-Reds want to "see" what they do. They need to achieve immediate and concrete results and also need to be in control of the outcome of their hard work. They enjoy clearly defined concepts or activities.

If Deep-Reds are in harmony they can be powerful workers and team players. Through their power, courage and strength, they are able to play an important part in their team or work environment. As long as they are able to balance their emotional temper and their physical power they will be accepted by their team.

Deep-Reds can solve their problems most effectively if they stay active and maintain a positive outlook and equally positive expectations. They possess enough physical stamina and energy to achieve virtually anything. Their physical bodies are considerably stronger than those of most other people. What they need to consider above all else is keeping an open mind, which is balanced with emotional clarity.

Having a positive outlook and positive expectations is important because Deep-Reds become impatient, angry and frustrated if things don't go well.

For Deep-Reds to achieve harmony and fulfillment in their lives they need to go beyond their basic survival mechanisms and physical activities and convert those drives into personal responsibility, creativity and a positive view of life.

Money translates into security, which in turn creates the means and ability to explore the physical reality. Otherwise, money has very little meaning to them. As long as they have the ability to make a decent living they will be happy and content.

Out of power Deep-Reds are often confronted with survival. They live a basic life style and sometimes have problems making enough money to survive. Their fear of survival and also the fear of death are the most dangerous blocks and difficulties for them to overcome. A positive perspective toward life and an awareness of their strong physical life energy gives them all the abilities they need to be successful.

Typical "Deep-Red" occupations would include: Mechanic, farmer, truck-driver, bartender, furniture mover, construction worker, bodyguard, policeman, firefighter, boxer or surgeon.

HEALTH, WELL-BEING AND GROWTH

To remain in harmony Deep-Red personalities must live and express their full potential. They need to find creative and practical ways of using their strength and physical power. Sports, building a house, fixing a car, working in the garden or other physical activities will help Deep Reds to tap into their creative power.

Because of their powerful physical energy, Deep-Reds cannot be told to relax or be passive. They need to understand the process of finding a harmonious expression for their intense power. They must find positive, growth oriented ways to express their powerful, explosive and intensive physical and emotional energy.

These outlets would preferably be found in sports, exercise, therapy or creativity. Their goal is to live their power in a creative way and release their frustrations without hurting themselves or others.

They also need to find a balance in their physical activities. Not allowing any relaxation or sensitivity toward their own feelings for long periods of time will deplete their life energy battery.

Deep-Reds also need to find and establish positive beliefs. Positivity and mental openness, combined with courage and physical strength, will assist them greatly in achieving their goals and desires. Positive thinking is very important. Even if life isn't perfect right now, having a positive outlook and attitude towards life will help Deep Red personalities in mastering their own life.

If Deep-Reds are able to share their inner feelings and open up for deeper communication, they will find a harmonious world of sensitivity and treasures. Remaining sensitive to their own true feelings and finding creative outlets of expression are valuable and important steps to free a Deep-Reds powerful life energy.

The first and most important step for a Deep-Reds is to take responsibility for their own life. The moment they make the conscious decision to change their inner focus from a basic survival mechanism to a sense of responsibility they will experience an incredible growth they could never have expected.

It is a matter of redirecting their powerful energy focus from fear, fight and survival, to positive, creative and entrepreneurial activities. When this occurs nothing can stop them, no matter which direction they may decide to go.

The moment a Deep-Red honestly decides to channel their energy into growth and expansion, their life will experience a tremendous shift towards success and happiness. Knowing there is more to life than physical, emotional expression and that everyone has to shape their own destiny, gives every Deep-Red enough positivity and understanding to make major changes in their own life.

Deep-Reds need to move their body. Not only watching sports but participating actively on a regular basis will help them tune into their creative, emotional power. All physical activities and sports combined with awareness and sensitivity are good and beneficial for Deep-Red personalities.

Practical applications and changes for a Deep-Red personality need to start with the physical body. It is obvious not only for Deep-Reds but all people that a rich and well-balanced nutrition is the basis for a healthy body/mind. Eating food that is light, low fat and rich in nutrients will not only release additional physical energy but also free toxins within the mind/body system.

RED PERSONALITIES

The following are the qualities and action words associated with RED personalities:

Area	Description
Physical	Physical vitality, energetic, movement, powerful action, leader, practical, sexual, vital force, over activity.
Emotional	Excitement, passion, sensual, driven by their desire, confident, impulsive stimulation, explosive temper, anger.
Mental	Will power, competitive, will to win, excitement, direct.
Spiritual	God is physical reality and is reflected in every positive action.
Motivation	Success, winner, full and intense life.
Mission/ Vision	Experience and enjoy life in the Here and Now.
Growth	Explosive, expansion, with strength and persistence.
Exercise	body building, football, soccer, running all competitive and professional sports aerobics, jogging, dancing,
Recharge battery	Integrate will power with love, balance their physical and emotional expression, social and open behavior.
Communication	Intense, loud voice, forceful, fast communicators
Interaction	Impulsive, electric, explosive, powerful, exciting.
Relationships	Enjoyment, stimulation, in general short-lasting partnerships.
Social, Friends	Center of attention, very active and open.

Sex, Intimacy	Eroticism, aliveness, stimulation, excitement, passionate lovers.
Money	Security, sign of their success, physical influence and power.
Success	Do everything to be successful and win, success is power.
Occupation	Active, stimulating jobs with possibility to succeed and win.
Career	Leader, sales people, enterprising productivity, entrepreneurs.

MIND/BODY

Red personalities find great pleasure in expressing themselves through their sexuality and their physical body. They live their life in the Here and Now with strength, courage and confidence. Reality is tangible for them because they see, hear, feel and smell it. These personalities have a remarkably strong will power and they enjoy all physical aspects of life. Reds are powerful, energetic and are often found in cooperative enterprises or leadership positions.

Reds perceive life through physical reality and through action. Their primary motivation is to feel alive and strong. They are constantly looking for excitement and judge their own environment and success by how powerful and competitive they are. Reds strive to be successful and are born winners. They are passionate about life. They represent the fire element: physical love, passion, heat and desire. The more excitement they experience the more alive they will feel.

Reds are practical, action-oriented, love to achieve results and be successful. They have an insatiable urge to win and create something valuable and important in their life. Their strong will power and intense, almost unlimited physical energy, allows them to be extremely active, persistent and successful in virtually anything they do.

Other people might sometimes experience a Reds power as overwhelming, their excitement, physical and emotional pressure as just, "too much".

Reds love to live in an exciting and stimulating atmosphere at work or in their private lives, which other people might consider to be filled with stress or tension. They have a tendency of pushing and forcing themselves to the maximum. They need to prove, mostly to themselves, that they can do anything and everything they want.

Reds are truly social people. They enjoy just hanging out with their friends and buddies. A typical idea of having a good time might include dancing all night, celebrating virtually anything with friends or spending a passionate night with their lover.

While Reds may be open and communicative, they are not very effective when it comes to talking about their deep inner feelings. They have not learned to talk about or share their deepest secrets. Being sensitive and clear is an essential step towards a free expression of their inner self. Reds experience the many emotions and feelings in their physical body. They are very sensual beings.

In harmony Reds are energetic, optimistic, honest and loyal. They outwardly radiate strength and persistence and have an intensive desire to live life to its fullest extent. A Red's purpose in life is to completely experience the physical world with joy, courage and energy. Reds can show humanity the power and strength of a human being.

Reds need a high degree of independence and physical freedom. They love to explore all facets of physical reality. They also enjoy the power and the thrill of exploration and adventure. Reds can be completely unique and individual. They generate so much passion and unconventional ways of expressing themselves that they sometimes have difficulty fitting into societies stereotyped picture of a normal citizen. However, Red personalities are used to this uniqueness and in fact, thrive on it. Strangely enough, they have a tendency of being loners who just happen to have lots of friends.

Reds are curious, insistent and intrusive. They are passionately interested in all aspects of life. If you desire a life filled with excitements and action, join forces with a Red personality. They have difficulty with exercising patience or waiting for projects to develop. They want everything immediately and are not afraid to insist that their ideas and goals are most important right now. Reds not only know how to get attention but also how to get what they want. Their powerful, physical-emotional energies, combined with driving, strong will power, gives them the right tools and instruments to be successful in our competitive, materialistic world.

Reds can become impatient and frustrated easily if things do not go their way. They feel more comfortable in taking physical action on a given situation rather than exploring vague, mental concepts. Learning by actually doing is a concept they are much more familiar with. It is easier for Reds to learn how to dance, to dismantle a car or to sell life insurance, if they can physically do it themselves. Classroom learning is not tangible for them. Structured instruction and most book learning situations require mental concepts that are not real or physically touchable.

Because powerful, physical and emotional energies are constantly running through a Reds body, it is difficult for them to sit still and be passive. The only way to achieve balance and harmony is to move the physical body and find ways of balancing this power inside. If Reds find positive outlets for their physical-emotional energy, they will become very powerful and will be able to manifest their dreams. Sports, which require physical stamina and strength, are wonderful outlets for Reds powerful, impulsive energies.

If Red personalities are out of harmony they might feel emotionally or physically exhausted. They can become frustrated, depressed or physical-emotional explosive. Out of power, their strong emotional and physical energies are often released through a physical fight, an intense sexual encounter or emotional burn out and exhaustion.

It is difficult to be around an out-of-power Red because they can be demanding, intense, explosive and have a constant need to be the center of attention.

Unbalanced Reds can exhibit an intense, pushy and controlling personality. However, they may not be aware of it because their constant, fast action and their need to win and achieve, has a tendency of clouding their perceptions. They are unaware that others might not want to go along with that particular speed and power. Out of power Reds, without giving any thought to it, easily go over both their own and other peoples feelings, borders and limits.

Reds will listen to spiritual or mystical subjects but they are much too grounded in their own realism to understand or accept these thoughts. On the other hand, Reds might occasionally see the excitement and power of spirituality when based in religion and decide to find out what this is really all about.

Because of their passionate energy, their will power and their urge to be in the front seat, Reds can become powerful leaders. A Reds spirituality is tangible. They might perceive God as a powerful human being who is in control and knows how to guide human life. On the other hand, Reds are too eccentric and unorthodox to be caught in organized religion.

SOCIAL LIFE

Reds are social personalities. They love people and love to be around people. Socializing and just hanging out with their friends, buddies, lovers or partners is a favorite activity of Reds. They will easily find friends and people to talk to wherever they go. They have a tendency of radiating an aura of attraction and excitement around themselves. At parties Reds are usually the center of attention. They enjoy being surrounded by beautiful men or women.

Their vibrant, energetic and stimulate personality, combined with power and vitality, makes them fun to be with. Reds love to interact with their environment and are interested in hearing other people's opinions and thoughts.

Reds can be eccentric and unique. Because of their strong physical and emotional creativeness, they often have difficulty in conforming with the norms of society. Their unusual behavior, as an example, the way they sometimes dress, can occasionally be shocking to a society based in conservatism.

Reds are sensitive and easily hurt. But they don't ever want to show their sensitivity. They are also very emotional. They need to express their feelings and emotions to experience peace and harmony inside themselves. Similar to Greens, Red personalities express their emotions and feelings very naturally. Like sensual animals, they have to get rid of this impulsive, intense powerful energy. And, they have to express these feelings through their physical bodies.

Communication is not a Reds favorite activity though they are powerful communicators. They prefer social or business meetings to sophisticated, intellectual conversations. Even if Reds do like parties or large get-togethers, they are careful with whom they get involved. They usually only open up to their long-time friends or people they know they can trust. Reds like people who understand their desires and goals.

RELATIONSHIPS AND INTIMACY

Reds are sexual beings and have a strong appetite for life. They love to be physically and emotionally stimulated and equally love to stimulate others. If you ask a Red person, they will commit to thinking about sex a great deal of the time. They are driven by their desires. They also love to confront and shock their fellow people just to see their reactions and emotional response. Sex means life to Reds. It is the essential force in their universe. Reds have difficulties in going without sex for a long time. They need this exciting and alive feeling of sexual interaction.

Sex for these realists is a desire-filled, sensual and lusty experience. Life in a physical body is to be fully enjoyed in every aspect. They love to openly express their desires, their sensuality and their passion. However, sex doesn't always involve love and compassion, but is a physical pleasure to be enjoyed and experienced.

It is a major challenge for a Red personality to live in a sensitive, long-lasting, emotional and open relationship. They often focus on short-term, exciting relationships and encounters. Reds have a lot of friends, but only a few are close and intimate. Because of their sexual power, Reds are often good candidates for affairs. They prefer the romantic feeling of the initial attraction and the excitement of meeting a new partner. They love to play with fire.

Because of their sexual drive, Reds are not very monogamous. They just can't help it. Their sexual power attracts too many good-looking women or men. A Red will feel a sexual orgasm as the highest of experiences. For them it is almost the same as spiritual enlightenment.

Reds love to go out with their friends, dance all night long and hang out in bars or clubs. They do not make perfect husbands or wives. If they have the courage to engage themselves in a close relationship they need physical freedom from their partners. If passion, sex and excitement are present in their relationship, Reds make very honest and loyal partners.

Reds are often attracted to Color Personalities in their own color range (Deep-Red, Red, Orange). Reds like the excitement and stimulation of love. This physical and sexual excitement will create many attractions, but on the other hand will also create many conflicts. Intimacy and deeper understanding are often difficult to achieve.

Reds interacting with Reds is often like an explosion or burning fires competing with each other. However, they seem to be very good mirrors for each other. Yellows add to a Reds sexual and physical power by being playful and fun.

The Orange adventurer and the Red winner both need a lot of time for themselves. Therefore, close relationships need a lot of space and understanding for each other.

To achieve productive relationships Reds need to understand the Blues, Indigos, Lavenders and Whites sensitivity and need for inner peace for successful interactions.

Reds seem to be attracted to Green and Deep-Green personalities because of their mental quickness, elegance and inner power. Because of their visionary and innovative traits, Violets match well with Reds though a lot of sensitivity is needed. A Violets passion and vision and a Reds physical approach can create miracles on earth.

In general, Red personalities need to understand that other people are not as powerful and ambitious as they are. Sensitivity and awareness toward other people's feelings will help to create long-lasting, fulfilling relationships.

CAREER AND FINANCE

It is virtually impossible to stop a Red if they have decided to go for and achieve a goal. They are powerful in achieving and finishing projects. They lead others through their powerful physical willingness to act and work and through the sheer essence of their will power. For a Red, "No" is not an acceptable answer. "No", simply means you haven't tried hard enough.

Reds do not lead with strategy or vision, but with courage and power. Reds can best solve their problems if they stay active and act powerful with positive expectations and ideas. They do not like sitting around discussing theories. Reds come up with creative, sometimes unusual ideas, but they also want to be physically involved in solving the problems at hand. Having both a positive outlook and positive expectations is very important for them.

Reds are not very patient when it comes to finding solutions or solving problems. If things don't go their way they might become impatient, angry or frustrated with themselves or close friends. Reds need to have things "their" way, which often creates frictions in a team environment.

However, if they stay emotionally and mentally open, they can be very creative and powerful problem solvers. Reds are especially good in finishing projects. Wherever stamina, courage and strength are required, Reds are welcome helpers.

Once they have firmly decided on a direction, Reds need to learn to accept other options and solutions. Being stubborn and inflexible isn't always positive or helpful to them in achieve a goal. The more flexible and discriminative they can be, the better they will understand where to change directions and push various projects to successful conclusions.

Money is an important issue to Reds mainly because it represents power in our society. They know how to work and make a good income. Reds often own their own businesses or are found in leadership positions. Their motivation is the money they make and the action and the excitement they experience.

Reds are independent personalities. They do not like to be told what to do, when to do it or what to believe in. They often choose occupations, which allow them to be their own boss and express their own ideas as an individual. They want to control and be the master of their own life. Reds enjoy working for themselves, being alone and focusing on their work. They do best if they have a clear picture of what to achieve and are then given the freedom to find the best and most efficient way for themselves.

Red personalities prefer physical work, which allows them the opportunity to achieve their own goals and win. They have a deep seeded desire to be the best and will do "whatever it takes" to accomplish their goals. They have a need to be in control of their work and their life. Competition and the excitement of interesting jobs are good motivational factors for Reds.

Because of their will to achieve and to finish projects, Reds can be vitally important in any work environment.

Typical "Red" occupations would include: Entrepreneur, sports professional, sales person, marketing executive, manager, surgeon, leader, athlete, dancer, and model.

HEALTH, WELL-BEING AND GROWTH

Reds have tremendous physical and emotional energies. If they learn how to find positive outlets for their powerful force and if also learn how to channel their life energy into creative projects and positive actions, they will be very successful and happy individuals.

To remain in harmony Red personalities must live and express their full potential. They must find positive avenues to express their powerful, explosive and intensive energy, such as sports, exercise, work or creativity. They must also learn to live their power in a creative way and release their intense physical and emotional energies without hurting themselves or others.

If Reds can learn to be sensitive enough to feel their own and others peoples feelings they will experience more love and acceptance in their lives. Reds cannot be told to relax, be passive or to just not do anything. They have too much power and energy A good way to let go and relax is to "hang loose", while involved in an activity. I would call this, "centered awareness in action", or "relaxed activity".

Physical activities and sports are wonderful ways to express their powerful energies. Jogging, swimming and dancing will help them to relax. Reds often experience this relaxation much like it was a psychedelic or a high experience. Reds also need to understand that winning isn't everything in life. They will often feel a certain emptiness after they have achieved their goals. "What is next?," they might ask themselves. Finding the "right" goal is an important issue for Red personalities.

Reds recharge their life energy batteries by finding creative ways of expressing physical activities. They can effectively learn to not suppress their feelings but to stay sensitive and open and express them creatively. Enough physical and emotional energy is available for Reds. Unlike other color personalities, Reds don't need to recharge themselves in a normal sense. Reds represent fire. Living filled with passion and developing a positive outlook with positive expectations will guide Reds toward a fulfilling and energetic life.

<u>ORANGE</u> PERSONALITIES

The following are the qualities and action words associated with ORANGE personalities:

Area	Description
Physical	Adventurous, physical, creative, thrill energetic, love to form shape and challenge physical reality, excitement.
Emotional	Happiness, pleasure, positivity, strength, sympathetic, enjoyment of physical reality, self confident, curiosity. inner pressure.
Mental	Creative, plans, strategies, productive, ambitious, challenge, control, need for action, conviction, tensions.
Spiritual	Experience peace and bliss in their adventures or creative projects.
Motivation	Adventurer, thrill of experience, ambitious to achieve goals, excitement or adrenaline rush they'll receive from their actions.
Mission/ Vision	To live their creative potential with pleasure and enjoyment.
Growth	Step-by-step, planned, powerful, strong.
Exercise	Adventurous, outdoor activities, mountain climbing, racing, surfing.
Recharge battery	Relaxation of mind and body, harmonious creative expression, enjoy life, let go.
Communication	Forceful, direct and creative, loud voice.
Interaction	Strong and powerful, goal oriented, often pushy and forceful.
Relationships	Companionship, independent individuals, appear self-centered.
Social, Friends	Physical and mentally attractive characters, few close friends.

Sex, Intimacy	Fun and pleasure, physical exercise and release, non-commitment.
Money	Needed for adventures and projects, possibly to be creative.
Success	Level of pleasure and creativity, achieve their own goals.
Occupation	Free-lance, need physical freedom and independence.
Career	Found in business, marketing, sales, boss, organizer, entrepreneur.

MIND/BODY

Orange personalities are the creative adventurers in the color spectrum. They have an inner urge to be creative, active and enjoy life to its fullest. They are also individual and independent and integrate physical and mental qualities. They enjoy the challenge and excitement of forming and shaping physical reality. Orange personalities love to imagine and plan strategies for their next adventure or project and then put those plans into action. They need to be involved in the actual working process and want to physically shape and form their own ideas. They have difficulty sitting back and letting other people do things for them. They are always busy building, organizing and shaping their projects and physical reality.

An Orange personalities motivation in life is based on how much pleasure and satisfaction they get out of their own adventures, challenges and creative projects. They want to be adventurous, creative and live out their own ideas.

Oranges mainly live within their own heads. But in contrast to a Yellow-Brown personality, they can't sit by idly and watch others make things happen. They have too much physical power to create, shape and form their own ideas and projects.

They plan and prepare their creative projects extremely well because they want to challenge themselves and others. They want to show themselves that they can achieve the results they were aiming for.

Conquering and overcoming the obstacles of the impossible, either within their own mind or within physical reality, is primarily what they are looking for. They also need to convince others of their abilities to be in control of their own success. For these creative adventurers, life is real, concrete and tangible.

Oranges have a need to be in charge of their own physical, emotional and mental reality. Letting go would mean to lose control. The processes of letting go and relaxation are not preferred Orange qualities. It is difficult for them to sit still and relax their body or their mind. Oranges are either physically or mentally active all the time. The two primary outlets for their adventurous energy are to be creative from either a physical or a mental standpoint.

Physical Orange personalities channel their energy into adventures and pleasures of the physical world. They thrive on excitement, adventure, thrill and danger. They enjoy challenging and conquering all facets of physical reality, to "boldly go where no one has gone before."

They love to discover their own physical limitations and then expand upon them. Many Orange personalities will create unusual, risky and often dangerous situations for the purpose of feeling more alive. They love the rush of adrenaline when faced with danger or death. The prospect of having a family sounds very conservative to these adventurers. Philosophies and concepts of spirituality are mainly empty talk and have little or no meaning.

Many Orange personalities were found in the past, especially in the pages of history where physical adventure and courage were needed for survival. Traveling into new territories, discovering new lands and conquering nature or other nations was the way of living.

In today's civilized society these qualities are not needed as much as they were back then. This would explain why most Orange personalities channel their energies into physically creative projects and a series of adventures.

A large percentage of Orange personalities channel their stimulating and exciting energies into mental and creative activities rather than physical activities and adventures. They are active with their minds and apply their fresh ideas into physical reality. They enjoy working on new, daring enterprises and projects, which promise to be challenging, exiting and adventurous. These courageous people love to do business, create companies, sell and market products, plan and generate strategies and organize and work out deals. They are not afraid of going into the details or doing the necessary work, but they prefer to stimulate and energize their ideas and projects. It is important for them to be actively involved, to get things going.

If they are in harmony and their personality is balanced, Oranges can be inventive and filled with creative ideas. They love the planning and creating of new strategies for their next physical or mental adventure. They live their life on a physical and creative level with power and confidence. Oranges who are in harmony have found a way to express themselves and channel their strong creative energies into positive projects and activities.

Orange personalities have the capacity to mentally tune into other people's minds or into virtually any situation they may wish to conquer. They also have the ability to figure out what patterns, risks and advantages are involved in those same situations. This ability to tune into and understand other peoples thinking is widely used, especially in the areas of sales and marketing. However, it is not uncommon for this same ability to be strongly misused as well.

If you ask Orange people they will agree that it is difficult for them to feel peaceful, quiet or calm. It is also extremely difficult for them to stop their thinking or planning process. Their physical and mental energies are very powerful and sometimes create an inner pressure, an urge to express and create.

Many Oranges integrate physical and mental creativity. They love to plan, organize and develop new devices or ideas. Then they want to form and shape those ideas until the stage where they can bring them into physical reality. They have a need to be involved in the active creation of their ideas.

Orange people love physical activities, which are thrilling and exiting. They enjoy sports such as surfing, parachute gliding, mountain climbing and other similar action filled events. They need the excitement, pleasure and fulfillment provided by physical movement and adventure.

They prefer individual, competitive sports to organized, team sports or challenges. Oranges often feel uncomfortable if they can't move their bodies or find themselves engaged in the wrong type of activity.

If an Orange personality is out of balance they can be egotistical, jealous and self centered. They are only interested in their own actions and ideas, no matter what effects this might have on others. They often show no affection, caring or compassion and can be distant, cold and aloof.

In business, and especially sales, you might regularly be confronted with out-of-power Orange personalities. Because they are not connected to their creative power, they try to manipulate, control and overpower others. On occasion they will try to find a "cheap" way of achieving results and success. They use their powerful courage and adventurous energy to compensate their disconnection with both themselves and their creativeness.

Orange personalities have problems relaxing both physically and mentally enough to adequately get to know themselves. They have difficulties in recognizing who they are emotionally, mentally and spiritually.

The primary confrontation for Orange personalities is to honestly accept the biggest challenge of them all: The adventure of self-discovery. This challenge needs more courage than all other outside physical activities combined. Unbalanced Oranges also have problems with being sensitive and caring toward their fellow human beings.

Oranges have a tendency of believing that spirituality and religion are concepts, which need to be lived in the physical world. In addition they have a physical perception of God. They believe that shaping and creating the planet earth and their own reality by their own will is a God given gift. Oranges understand and live this concept and belief.

The primary goal of an Orange personality is to enjoy life, have fun and be creative. The only time they come close to experiencing God or Spirit is in a state of ecstasy or thrill. Whenever Oranges are fully in the "here and now", they will have a spiritual and enlightening glimpse of reality.

SOCIAL LIFE

Orange personalities are not very social people. They prefer to live in their own world of adventure, thrill and excitement and to lose themselves in their own creative projects. They don't particularly care what others or society in general thinks about them. Nor do they take those thoughts very personally if they are considered to be egotistical, self-absorbed or self-centered. They have not asked for any attention or justification, they simply want to do their own thing.

Oranges don't necessarily follow the rules of society. They are actually the people who constantly try to expand and exceed societies or others personal expectations, limitations and restrictions. Their bodies and minds are designed to conquer all physical limitations and boundaries. In today's society, these particular qualities are not needed as much as they obviously were several decades ago.

Therefore, it is important for Orange personalities to find adequate outlets and channels of expression for their powerful creativity.

Communication is not a high priority item for Oranges. However, they do possess the capacity to clearly explain and get across to others exactly what they want. When it comes to their ideas and projects, they do know how to communicate and do it most effectively. But if we look closely at their emotional expression, their ability to communicate their inner feelings, we find insecurity, unavailability and even a sense of loneliness.

RELATIONSHIPS AND INTIMACY

Orange personalities are loners. They don't need friends or partners in their lives. They feel more alive and happy if they have succeeded in a large project or while they are involved in a major, physical adventure. From an emotional standpoint they have difficulty in bonding. They also have a tendency of not relating well to sensitivity, compassion and gentleness.

For the most part Oranges are normally not interested in solid, long-lasting partnerships or relationships. They are more interested in their projects and adventures than in family and marriage. Because they are physically fit, attractive and good looking, Orange people have no difficulty in finding partners and lovers. The challenge, excitement and pleasure of meeting new people is much more thrilling than simply being together with old friends all the time.

Oranges enjoy all pleasures of the physical body. They consider sexuality as a natural body reaction. It is fun for them, a nice release from inner pressures. But in their hearts they do not care or are affected very deeply by their partner. It is a challenge for Orange personalities to become emotionally involved and take on the responsibilities of a relationship. If they can feel enough freedom and independence they might be willing to commit to a partner for a longer period of time.

But their partners will soon discover that they can't confine or hold back an Oranges urge to challenge further adventures. Orange people can be interesting, thrilling and fascinating, but they need their freedom to explore and create their own life.

Orange people interacting with other Oranges or Reds often create an intense and high-energy relationship. Friction and ego problems are not unusual. Deep-Reds and Oranges seem to have similar interests and are very compatible. Orange personalities like a Yellows playfulness. Both are very creative and productive and therefore have a great deal in common.

The Orange adventurers need a lot of time for themselves. Therefore close relationships are not their first priority. They usually have problem with the Blues need for closeness and caretaking. Both Orange and Indigo personalities seem to have strong inner feelings and creativity yet they live in a completely different world - almost inside out. Because Greens and Deep-Greens love to talk about everything for hours, Oranges might need some time off.

Creating sensitivity and understanding for Lavender and White personalities is a strong challenge for most Oranges. An Oranges practicality and a Violets theoretical visions seem to support each other very well. On the other hand, Violets are often too far out for an Orange person.

In reality the biggest challenge for an Orange personality is to create relationships that are ruled by sensitivity and understanding. To open their heart is a wonder not to be missed.

CAREER AND FINANCES

Orange people are independent and self-sufficient individuals. They prefer short term or individual jobs to long-time commitments or safe occupations. They don't have much of a problem with money.

Because their needs are not very high and they have the power to be creative and active, they have the abilities to create their own income without too much difficulty. If they have the chance, Oranges will love to live the physical, adventurous and thrilling life and find a way of making money with it.

Oranges primarily spend their money for their unusual projects or hobbies. They don't need much in the form of luxury but they are more than willing to spend anything, and in some cases, everything they have, to make their ideas a reality.

Oranges can be strong leaders, but they actually don't care about being leaders at all. They prefer going their own way, fulfilling their own dreams of creative adventures. They can be powerful and creative leaders if they see the necessity of working with other team members. They perform best in an environment, which provides them a certain degree of freedom and independence. Oranges lead by physical example and by their unbridled enthusiasm. Their "male" way of living their life creates many admirers and followers.

Orange personalities are creative problem solvers. They are able to view and recognize all factors, calculate the risks involved, go through all possibilities in their head, and make sure they have all the equipment they need and then take action. They prefer physical or mental challenges and are often found in jobs, which guarantee them a degree of independence. Oranges are often found in business, sales, marketing or any other occupation, which allows them to experience personal freedom.

Orange personalities are qualified and strong working people. They love to express their powerful creative life energy into many avenues. Whenever a strong, fearless personality with courage, enthusiasm and determination is needed, look for an Orange person.

Typical "Orange" occupations are: Stunt men, mountain climbers, adventurers, business men, sales persons, designers, developers, architects, explorers and private investigators.

HEALTH, WELL-BEING AND GROWTH

Orange personalities need to understand that to explore the inner worlds is the greatest adventure a human being can experience. To take the journey into their inner reality, explore this unknown land and to expand their consciousness, is the biggest challenge they will ever face.

Orange persons reach harmony if they recognize that their life needs balance, a balance of body, mind and spirit. To explore the outer as well as the inner world enables them to experience life on all levels. The moment they connect in a balanced manner with their inner, creative power. Oranges will know what to do and what not to do.

Inner Knowledge and Wisdom can be achieved if the creative energies flow freely and are expressed to help and support humanity. Connecting with their own feelings and staying open and caring toward humanity are vitally important aspects for Oranges.

Orange personalities recharge their batteries if they live their creative capacity in a harmonious way. They must understand how unimportant it is to force themselves into dangerous experiences or unhealthy situations. By using their power to create and help others and to experience their inner world of sensitivity, feelings and personal growth, they will find positive and harmonious ways of expressing and recharging themselves.

The life purpose of an Orange personality is to connect with their creative potential and experience the entire physical existence. Further, it is to have the freedom to create new pathways and ideas and to expand and go over the borders and limitations of reality, as it is commonly perceived.

Orange personalities need to be especially aware about their physical and emotional states. Proper, healthy and high-energy nutrition is essential for them. They should also create an environment in which they can express themselves emotionally and communicate freely with friends and family.

Sports such as surfing, mountain climbing, riding a horse or a Harley Davidson through the desert or other outdoor activities and adventures are known to recharge an Orange personalities battery. On the other hand, the biggest challenge for them is to find their limits where adventure and independence become destructive and a form of energy drain.

YELLOW-BROWN PERSONALITIES

The following are the qualities and action words associated with Yellow-Brown personalities:

Area	Description
Physical	Grounded, focused on own reality, physical stamina, determination, endurance, form and shape physical reality, creative.
Emotional	Strength, stability, patience, mental playfulness, emotional suppression, conservative, control, withdrawn.
Mental	Logical, analytical, intellectual, detail oriented, patterns, order, structure, stability, stubborn, single-minded.
Spiritual	Study of higher wisdom, spiritual laws and order, God is thought.
Motivation	Mental pleasure and creativity, detailed work and results.
Mission/ Vision	Experience life in details, emotional openness and sensitivity.
Growth	Detailed, step-by-step, precise, slow.
Exercise	Jogging, bicycling, swimming.
Recharge battery	Mental relaxation, focus, connect with their intuition, trust inner feelings and guidance.
Communication	Slow expression, detailed communication, think first, then talk.
Interaction	Cautious, prefers safe environment and life, love discussions.
Relationships	Roots, home, familial security, aloof, companionship, caretaking.
Social, Friends	Community service, close to family, friends, deep commitments.

Sex, Intimacy	Loyal, secure, stable partners, conservative habits and customs.
Money	Security conscious, plan in great detail, represents safety, control.
Success	How precise, detailed and perfect they think and perform.
Occupation	Very precise in work and expression, conservative and conventional.
Career	Supervision, middle management, precise problem solving.

MIND/BODY

Yellow-Browns are logical, analytical, detail oriented and creative personalities. They are sequential thinkers and carefully process every step they take. They have a basic need to understand and analyze each individual step before continuing on to the next level.

Yellow-Browns strongest qualities are their clear intellectual and analytical properties. They like to create a solid foundation, which gives them security, and then build stone by stone until they eventually achieve their goals. Virtually everything they do contains logic and methodology. They are constantly planning, trying to figure out how to reach the requirements of their goal.

A Yellow-Browns motivation in life is their need to know and to analytically and intellectually understand life and interact with other people. Their guiding sentence could be, "Life is like a computer. You get out of it what you program into it".

Yellow-Browns mainly process life through their minds. They don't use their body and emotions nearly as much as most other color personalities. They perceive nature or physical reality first through their analytical mind and then move toward action.

Physical activities are not important to them. They have a tendency of only moving their body if they find a good reason and are convinced about the benefits involved.

If Yellow-Brown personalities are in harmony, they radiate stability, security and responsibility towards their fellow beings. They are the most dependable people in the world who fulfill all tasks to the smallest detail with extreme efficiency. Through their rational and practical abilities they can realize visionary ideas of other personality types and bring them into reality. Yellow-Browns have a soothing and stabilizing effect on people and they are trustworthy and reliable. They also express strong security and groundedness and are considered to be realistic people.

Yellow-Browns are known to examine the details of everything, they do. When they work on a project they need to see and understand all of its components before they feel safe and secure enough for their participation. Sometimes Yellow-Browns may not be able to see the whole picture because they are too intensely involved with the details. But for them that doesn't matter. Their unbelievable patience and tolerance allows them to spend many hours on the same idea or project.

Yellow-Browns love to play and tinker with electronic gadgets, cars, motorcycles, etc. If they become involved with a project or hobby they go into every detail and in most cases become experts in their field. Through patience, obstinacy and their love for detail, Yellow-Browns have developed appliances such as computers, radios and other technical appliances.

In both expression and communication, Yellow-Browns are slow and deliberate. They will divide and describe every situation in its smallest detail. They speak preferentially about their thoughts, ideas and projects. Yellow-Browns are also careful in expressing their deepest feelings and emotions. They will only open up and share their innermost feelings with others after they are convinced no one will hurt them or use information against them.

Yellow-Browns love to study and to learn. They make perfect students because they are willing to spend the time, effort and energy to understand the smallest of details. Sometimes this positive ability creates problems because only seeing reality as orderly, structured and rigid, doesn't give them the necessary openness to expand themselves and explore unknown territories.

Yellow-Brown personalities have specific ideas and concepts about life. They don't like things, which strike them as unusual, extra-ordinary, abnormal or irregular. These security conscious people can easily become accustomed to old and repeated family or life patterns. Their normal day would proceed with definite patterns, situations and regularity. As an example, at 10 PM every evening they watch the news, their office desk always looks exactly the same, organized, every item at its place, the same dinner every Tuesday night.

It is often difficult for them to go new ways, to accept new ideas or patterns or to encounter the unexpected. However, this lifestyle, connected to security, solidity and comfort is attractive to many people. Yellow-Browns qualities and characteristics are appreciated and sought after by many people in the business world and society.

Out-of-power Yellow-Browns can be stubborn, stuck, narrow-minded and extremely skeptical about all things. They can be overly analytical with a need to understand everything and to mentally be in control. Whatever they can't prove or don't know represents insecurity, instability and therefore danger. Their skepticism does not allow different opinions or points of view. Even when proof stares them in the face they can be overly stubborn, skeptical and totally unwilling to change or alter their positions or beliefs.

Yellow-Browns who are unbalanced mainly think about or talk about their feelings. However, they hardly ever feel them in the real sense. As an example, even trained experts such as psychologists or therapists understand emotional concepts mentally, but have difficulty in experiencing living out their own emotions and feelings. Yellow-Browns withdraw emotionally in stress situations and then try to analyze and discuss the situation within themselves until they come up with solutions.

A Yellow-Browns primary difficulty is making contact with their own emotions and feelings. Their personality will not allow them to feel something, which cannot be analyzed and figured out completely. How do you define or understand feelings and emotions like love, anger or sadness?

Yellow-Browns are afraid of their own emotions and feelings because they justify that the universe cannot be reduced to mind, logic and intellect. This extremely deep rooted fear and insecurity goes so far that they solve most of their problems with known, safe and tried patterns. They will repeat and feel safe with known and established solutions because their parents, friends or superiors have always done things the same way.

Because they don't really know how to handle their emotions, Yellow-Brown personalities often suppress them and tell themselves these emotions do not exist. They create ways to eliminate emotion in their lives. If they can't accept and therefore express their feelings, they tend to become even more uninvolved, withdrawn and cold toward others.

Many Yellow-Browns turn their rage, anger or sadness inside, leaving them painfully in a depressed, hopeless, discouraged state of mind.

In general, Yellow-Brown personalities experience difficulty in relaxing or calming themselves. For them, letting go, no-mind and no thought is comparable to insecurity and even death. They perceive themselves as mind and thought and the moment the mind ceases to function they fear they don't exist anymore.

To remove themselves from this wicked circle, Yellow-Browns need to understand that emotions and feelings are an important parts of a human system. Without emotions, feelings, intuitions, beliefs and spiritual ideas, humans would be only matter or similar to a computer. Adapting a mental concept that integrates openness to emotions and intuition is the first step for Yellow-Browns to grow and expand their possibilities.

Their sense of spirituality is to grasp and understand the higher laws and concepts of life. They have the capacity to comprehend spiritual knowledge and wisdom as a result of their skilled, analytical mind and preciseness. For Yellow-Browns, the universe works within certain laws and orders, all of which can be logically explained and understood. They will only accept magical, mystical ideas, or psychic and spiritual phenomena after they have been carefully examined and they are convinced it is real. For these reality conscious people, beliefs are based upon hands-on proof and the concept of, "seeing is believing."

Yellow-Browns prefer religious practices which offer specific laws, rules and regulations that offer security and safety. For them, spirituality is related to high ethical values, justice, principles, perfection and fairness. God remains a mental concept the ultimate thought. They can understand what God or Spirituality actually is but rarely feel it. The major challenges for Yellow-Browns is to allow their emotions to be felt and intuitions to be integrated into their mental concepts of life.

SOCIAL LIFE

In today's society Yellow-Brown personalities are highly respected and appreciated. They are reliable, trustworthy, always on time and share a common understanding with society and most people. Their behavior and beliefs are within the range of normality and generally have a conservative approach. Yellow-Browns are social because they enjoy being together with friends or interesting people. Often, they need to see a particular reason behind various social activities or get-togethers. These activities would include such things as business, sports or religion.

Yellow-Browns are often found in social groups, business groups or meetings. It is here where they can find friends and partners to both discuss and mentalize their work and/or ideas. Another sought out advantage of these groups is they are seldom focused on an intimate, emotional or personal level.

Whenever Yellow-Browns feel the need to confront themselves with an inner, personal situation, they will prefer to withdraw in silence or in some cases even physically leave the meeting.

Yellow-Brown personalities are social in the sense that they love to share and support communities and other social groups. They see the need to give something back because they feel a sense of security and peace within the confines and structure of society. Yellow-Brown people are often found as managers, officers or accountants of various social organizations.

RELATIONSHIPS AND INTIMACY

Yellow-Browns fully commit to their partners and take complete responsibility for their own, every day life. They mate primarily for the purpose of creating a safe and secure home where they can take care of their family and in turn their partner takes care of them. They view love as a need to help and support, not as an emotional or passionate act.

Many people find themselves pulled toward Yellow-Brown personalities. Their stability and reliability are good pre-condition for long-lasting, cohesive, secure relationships. However, if you are looking for passion, romance and excitement, you should definitely make the effort to find a different partner. Yellow-Browns, for the most part, find "romance" to be much too practical and rational.

Contrary to the sense of involvement and personal responsibility they assume, it is fairly difficult for Yellow-Browns to become emotionally or spiritually involved. They prefer quiet moments in which they can read, learn, think or focus on their own ideas or projects. Out-of-power Yellow-Browns often feel unappreciated, especially during conversations when they feel they are not getting the attention they deserve. As a result they have learned to internalize their ideas or only share them with people who are on their own level of understanding.

Any person searching for intellectual conversations, quiet and rational thoughts, relationships based on partnership, stability and financial security will find great comfort in being with a Yellow-Brown personality.

Yellow-Browns usually like to be around Deep-Red and Deep-Green people. They have a lot in common and share a conservative and intellectual approach towards life. Yellow-Browns surely understand and relate easily with their own personality type. However, they also need to be careful to develop other color qualities in their life.

Yellow-Brown people are often attracted to a Yellows happiness and lightness and the adventurous and powerful expression of Red and Orange personalities. Blues and Indigos seem to be too emotional to match with Yellow-Browns. But, because they are like energetic counterparts they can learn tremendously from each other. As long as Yellow-Browns stay open for new and innovative ideas they are a good match with Violet personalities.

Yellow-Browns need to understand and accept the spiritual way of life which Lavender and White personalities prefer. Often they are too far out and therefore have difficulty in creating harmonious relationships with them.

CAREER AND FINANCES

Yellow-Browns prefer safe and secure jobs. They do not want to worry about their monthly or weekly income. If they don't have this sense of security they will feel uncomfortable and uneasy. It is quite common for them to pursue occupations or positions with large, established companies or organizations who can provide this security and regular income.

Yellow-Browns will be the right choice in any situation in which preciseness, detailed and analytical thinking is required. They can be extremely successful if they use their full capacity.

Their openness and willingness to discuss and analyze work situations and problems allow them to work well with other people. They lead by their competence, their ability to listen and unify, and uniqueness in being able to find the best solution for virtually any problem.

Yellow-Browns solve problems through logical and analytical procedures. If detailed, orderly and precise solutions are needed, they are extremely good problem solvers. However, they are not very effective when it comes to developing innovations or new ideas, making broad plans, or creating strategies, which incorporate complex or intuitive ideas or concepts. If they keep an open mind when looking into creative, new possibilities, they will be able to solve all problems in an efficient, practical and detailed manner.

Typical "Yellow-Brown" occupations are: Architects, bookkeepers, computer experts, software programmers, bankers, technicians, researchers, scientists, doctors, office clerks, library employees, officials, electricians and engineers.

HEALTH, WELL-BEING AND GROWTH

One of the first steps for Yellow Brown personalities to achieve balance in their life is to open up emotionally, to start feeling both their own and other peoples emotions. It takes, and calls for, a great deal of courage to go deep within oneself and allow these emotions to emerge. This emotional openness and sensitivity will allow them to use not only their mind, but in addition, the deep-seeded power of emotions.

After Yellow-Browns understand the primary need of getting in contact with their emotions and feelings, they will begin to see that intuition is an important aspect of life. Intuition means living with an open mind and looking at new, innovative ideas without skepticism. It also calls for having the willingness to explore their potentials. To gain harmony Yellow-Browns must recognize that their skepticism originates from insecurity and fear of change. They must learn to advance into new areas and be open for changes without always having data, statistics and facts available. They must also remain flexible and be willing to take risks.

Nearly all inventions and innovations have been created and developed by people with open minds and intuitive abilities. Yellow-Browns can be extremely successful and play an important part in society as long as they stay emotionally and mentally open. Yellow-Browns will go beyond their fear of insecurity if they understand that their mind is only a part of them. They need to clearly comprehend that their mind is not in control. Rather, they are in control of their own mind. With this understanding they will begin to relax their mental processes enough to more deeply explore their own personal identity.

The first step for Yellow-Browns to grow and expand their power is to make slow yet profound changes in their life. They need to understand that the only constant in the universe is change. To make physical, emotional or mental changes doesn't mean being out-of-control. It simply indicates the necessity of accepting real responsibility. When Yellow-Brown personalities let go of their fear and connect with their inner guidance, intuition and their inner feelings, they will expand their life energy and become the powerful, spiritual beings they really are.

Yellow-Browns need to be aware of their life energy. They have to understand that as human beings we have several internal systems, which are equally important. These systems include but are not limited to: physical, electrical-energetic, emotional, mental-analytical, intuitive-feeling, and spiritual. Yellow-Browns often hold back most of their real inner power as a result of fear and out of insecurity. It is always easier to play it safe then it is to take chances. They recharge their batteries best if they stay mentally and emotionally open. Expressing their feelings and emotions clearly and freely will release tremendous powers from within.

Artistic and creative activities such as painting or singing are wonderful techniques to open up their emotional and spiritual energies. Meditations that calm and focus the mind can help them to go beyond thinking towards a universe of unlimited possibilities.

<u>YELLOW</u> PERSONALITIES

The following are the qualities and action words associated with Yellow personalities:

Area	Description
Physical	Sunny, playful, creative, fun, easy life style, physically active, creative, strong body awareness, sensitivity, energetic, restless.
Emotional	Humor, cheerful, suggestive, brightness, radiant, happiness, pleasure, enjoyment, spontaneous, sympathetic, addictive.
Mental	Creative, bright, intelligent, learning, need to be active, interest, egotistic, superficial, expansiveness, never want to grow up.
Spiritual	Mental philosophies, concepts, spirituality is a physical experience and play, reflected in love, joy, laughter.
Motivation	Give and experience joy, happiness, playfulness, creativeness.
Mission/ Vision	Enjoy life, be creative, stay light and bright, reflection of sunlight.
Growth	Spontaneous, through commitment, focus.
Exercise	Outdoors, all fun activities, sports, beach ball, swimming, surfing.
Recharge battery	Natural high through meditation, prayer, balanced physical exercise and sexual activity, physical body is guiding antenna.
Communication	Playful, light, creative, overwhelming, overflowing, fast voice.
Interaction	Physically and mentally active, easy life style, no deep commitments.
Relationships	Companionship, independent individuals, self-centered.
Social, Friends	Very social and attractive, many friends, but few close friends.

Sex, Intimacy	Fun and pleasure, non-commitment, very sexual.
Money	Necessity, secondary, earn, spend easily.
Success	Level of pleasure and creativity, achieve their own goals.
Occupation	Free-lance, need physical freedom and independence, enjoyment.
Career	Business, marketing, design, sports, artist, massage or healing field.

MIND/BODY

Yellows are the sunniest, happiest and most childlike personalities in the color-spectrum. "All I want to do is have some fun!" is a song which is a wonderful representation of Yellows and shows their easy going, light and sunny character. These playful people have a wonderful sense of humor. They love to laugh and intimately enjoy life from many different angles. They advocate relaxation, the pure joy of life and live spontaneously. They are always reminding other people to not take life too seriously and to always look on the bright side. Life and work should both be enjoyed.

Yellows primary motivations are enjoyment, entertainment and creativity. They measure life by how happy and content they are and how good they feel. "Life is like a box of chocolates, it is sweet and a lot of fun."

Yellows are intelligent, bright and radiant personalities. They learn easily and receive information without asking about the deeper connections or reasons behind it. They love to work with their minds and equally love to play and occupy themselves with philosophies, mental ideas and concepts. They also enjoy discussing all aspects of life, from politics to spirituality.

Yellows can be spontaneous and overflowing with artistic and creative ideas. However, their focus is much more on enjoying than it is on creating. They create because it is fun and brings enjoyment, not because they want to achieve anything or reach any lofty goals. Yellows are kinesthetic and learn by doing. They will find that even though they are physically active they are also receptive for learning or receiving information.

They have an abundance of energy, which is easily recognized by their physical activeness. It is difficult for them to sit still for a long period of time. However, when this occurs, they have a constant need to be moving their hands. You might also find them unconsciously playing with a cigarette, playing with their napkin or making funny gestures with their hands. It is important for Yellows to stay fit. If they become frustrated, annoyed or furious, they need to express, direct and release their overflowing energies through their physical body.

In harmony Yellows are very creative. They love to work with their hands and enjoy doing such things as writing, painting, repairing things or sculpting. They know how to enjoy mental-creative and physical reality with all its variations. In balance Yellows are happy and content personalities. They inherently know how to accept whatever is happening in their lives. Yellows are the most child-like personalities in the color spectrum and they never want to grow up. As a result they generally look younger then they actually are. They love to travel, to see the world, to relax on a wonderful beach and have fun dancing all night long.

Yellows bodies are extremely sensitive. They are like antennas, sensing what other people feel or what vibes are emanating in a room. Their bodies are almost too sensitive and receptive for the volumes of information being generated by our high-tech society. As a result they have a tendency of overloading very quickly. They often don't understand why their body reacts so strongly to outside influences. They need to recognize these powerful reactions, these signs from their physical body, and then use this information as a tool for guidance in their life. Their physical bio-system senses the influence, reacts and then tells them what is happening.

You will immediately recognize if a Yellow is happy, sad or feels uneasy, because they emit unusually strong body language. A Yellow body never lies. It always shows the truth. They are sensitive and intuitive through their physical bodies and also through their touch. Therefore, Yellows are often found in occupations such as healing or massage. They love to be around people and they enjoy helping people. They have healing hands and a healing, light attitude towards life. All these qualities make Yellows excellent healers or therapists.

If Yellows are not connected to their overflowing, inner energy source or haven't learned how to channel their energy into positive creativity, they have no motivation at all and lean toward negative addictions. Out of power Yellows tend to be lazy and unmotivated, having no energy to live, to be creative or to enjoy life. They never want to grow up, preferring unlimited freedom rather than accepting terminal responsibility.

Yellow personalities have a fear of relationships, commitments and obligations. They will often run away from their problems and difficulties or simply ignore them. Various forms of running away could be expressed as constantly making excuses for things, sleeping all day long, being lethargic, being just plain lazy or continually moving from one location to another. Many Yellows are late on a regular basis. Even though they have difficulty in being on time they will always come up with creative and sufficient excuses.

Because of their sensitive, physical, bio-chemical bodies, Yellows do not like pain or even the thought of having to experience it. They will do nearly anything to avoid any form of discomfort.

Fun-loving Yellows are addictive and physically dependent personalities. They have a driving need to experience a physical "high" or an euphoric state of mind. If they focus on positive activities they remain energetic, joyful and creative. They receive an almost enlightened feeling by enjoying such activities as lying on the beach and being charged by the sunlight, physical exercise like jogging or bicycling, creating art or poetry or sexual stimulation culminating with orgasm. Yellows need movement, sex, sports or creativity.

Out-of-power Yellows will be drawn toward negative dependencies such as drugs, alcohol, cigarettes, caffeine, candies, overeating or unrealistic philosophies. At first they will feel good, even light, with a sense of release. However, soon depression, lethargy, apathetic and confused feelings and thoughts will surface. They need to change their focus from negative addictions toward positive and healthy activities. Because their bodies are so sensitive they will notice the effects of these negative addictions for a long time.

Yellows have a physical sense of spirituality. Their deepest spiritual experience is to enjoy life to its fullest and see God in everything. Happiness and love are signs of a living connection with the higher power, which most human beings refer to as God. Yellow personalities enjoy being involved with philosophies or other spiritual beliefs and concepts. They love to learn, be mentally creative and to understand God in its totality. Even so, they will seldomly commit toward a specific path or belief system.

SOCIAL LIFE

Yellow personalities are social people. They have many friends and are constantly looking forward to meeting new ones. They enjoy all varieties of get togethers. Yellows are welcome at any party because of their joyful, easy going and often funny attitude toward life and their intellectual brilliance. They are group conscious whether in organized, team sports or simply with their friends. They are typically the center of attention and seem to be surrounded by friends all the time. However, having many friends or at least knowing many people do not mean they are close or intimate with any of them.

Yellows enjoy a sense of sharing and communion through their constant physical activity and always being with several friends. Many of them passionately dislike being alone because they fear loneliness. However, being surrounded by friends does not necessarily indicate that this inner loneliness and emptiness will dissipate or ever go away.

Yellows need time for themselves to find their true inner self. Only by doing this will they find inner peace. Looking inside themselves will provide a sense of security, connectedness and the feeling of home. "Home is where your heart is".

A Yellow person can be easily recognized by their spontaneity, humor, and need to always be active and on the run. They are good friends, communicate openly with others and love to bring people together. For them, talking is just another way of creative expression and is something to be enjoyed. For the most part they are spontaneous in everything they do. You will find many Yellow personalities wherever fun and enjoyment are taking place.

RELATIONSHIPS AND INTIMACY

Yellows have a need for relationships. They can be sensitive and caring in both relationships and also partnerships. They prefer partners, who can laugh with them, support and take care of them, and will not challenge or take away their freedom. Yellow personalities have a deep seeded fear of commitment.

They want to be independent and free to enjoy everything life has to offer. As a result, many Yellows live as singles with unregular partners or in semi-committed relationships. On one hand they want intimacy and sexuality. On the other they fear that committing to only one partner might diminish or remove their options and freedom.

Yellows love to flirt and are emotionally charged by the excitement of meeting new and different people. For these addictive, color personalities the other sex is a way of connecting with life and also compensating for their own energy deficiencies.

They need to see and understand the differences between being independent, but loving and committed, and using a relationship as a substitute for their own problems.

Yellows are very sexual. Their foreplay can be considerate, playful and sensitive. Sexuality is as much an enjoyment as it is a physical relaxation and is felt as a whole body experience. Sexual sensations and orgasms create a sense of satisfaction, which cannot be compared with anything else.

Once they have experienced this feeling, which they view as a "sexual high', they want more and more. They need to make sure their relationships are balanced with both sexuality and intimacy. Sexual addiction only for the purpose of creating this high feeling will not make them happy in the long run.

Yellows love to be physically active and need a healthy but active sex life. Therefore they love to be around Red, Orange and Yellow personalities. Violets can add tremendous vision to a Yellows creativity. Blues are often too emotional and require commitment for a happy relationship.

Lavenders/Whites usually love to be around Yellows. Both of them love to discuss and become involved with spirituality or philosophy. Deep-Reds and Deep-Greens are often too conservative in their approach toward life.

Most Yellow personalities prefer being in a light, playful, intimate relationship without the emotional baggage of heavy commitments and lingering problems.

CAREER AND FINANCES

Yellows love being spontaneous, initiative and stimulative. They are the perfect selection for new projects but sometimes have difficulties finishing them. Money is not a primary issue for them. They can make money easily because they are not afraid to work hard. However, their money often goes out as quickly as it comes in.

Yellow personalities are creative problem solvers. They have the ability to create new, unusual and innovative solutions.

On the other hand, they also have difficulties in finishing projects or solving problems completely. They are good at starting things and keeping others enthusiastic. If they decide to take action and solve problems, Yellows will find simple, unique and inventive solutions. However, they often don't want to do the serious work, which is needed to accomplish or finish a project.

Yellows are good team members and lead others by example. They enjoy demonstrating and showing others how things work or how things could be done. They utilize their strong qualities of motivation and creativity. Yellows are the most likely of all the different personalities to have fun in their work or occupation.

Typical "Yellow" occupations are: Athlete, comedian, musician, painter, artist, student, philosopher, psychologist, massage therapist, health practitioner, waiter, mechanic, cook, stewardess or travel guide.

HEALTH, WELL-BEING AND GROWTH

Yellows need to take care of their physical bodies more then other color personalities. Their body is like an "energetic" antenna. They sense other people's feelings, thoughts or even vibrations in a room. If they do not stay in power their body will show imbalances and can be heavily effected by outside influences.

They also know exactly what the Mind/Body connection means. They are perfect examples of how emotions and thoughts influence and are interconnected with the physical body. Yellows will be considerably healthier if they learn to listen to both their physical antenna and their body/mind.

Yellows need to emotionally understand that commitments and relationships can help them reach deeper levels of intimacy and self-awareness. This same understanding will also bring more fun, excitement and freedom into their lives. Their problems will not simply disappear just by avoidance or running away from them. They can create successful solutions by confronting all aspects of life with joy and an easy attitude.

To achieve harmony in their life, Yellows need to find creative and playful ways of expression. Actively expressing their physical and creative energies will allow them to live an easy going, happy and joyful life. Positive addictions such as physical exercise and movement, healthy and playful sex or meditation and prayer are extremely important.

Activities like bicycling, tennis, dancing, jogging or other long-muscle exercises are recommended for Yellows and should be practiced daily.

Active meditations such as Dynamic Meditation, Qui-Gong or Tai Chi have positive effects because they focus the mind and connect the physical body with the universal energy flow. Yellows who are healthy and in power need a fulfilling sexual life to be connected with their abundant energy and enjoy all aspects of life.

GREEN PERSONALITIES

The following are the qualities and action words associated with GREEN personalities:

Area	Description
Physical	Mind/body balance, strong mind/body awareness, need to move their body, healthy, physically active individuals.
Emotional	Contentment, harmony, balance, open, friendly, natural expression of heart, strong roots, security conscious.
Mental	Quick, detailed thinking, verbal, high ideals and expectations, expression of thoughts, easily bored, conservative.
Spiritual	Nature is God, harmony and balance.
Motivation	Create balance, peace, harmony, need to teach and communicate.
Mission/ Vision	To enjoy life in harmony and balance, express themselves.
Growth	Natural process of growth, evolution, find goals and mission.
Exercise	Swimming, dancing, talking, walking with the dog, horseback riding.
Recharge battery	Need nature to recharge, walk in park or forest, play with animals, dancing, being lazy, lots of talking.
Communication	Fast, easy going teachers, love to share their thoughts and feelings.
Interaction	Easy going, open, light and superstitious.
Relationships	Family oriented, need few but close friends.
Social, Friends	Very social, need to communicate, interact.
Sex, Intimacy	Natural expression, alive, love, affection.

Money	Luxury, clothing, gifts, vacations, spend money easily, security.
Success	Harmony, expression and interaction with others is more important than being ambitious or having high goals.
Occupation	Need people to interact with, born teachers and communicators.
Career	Teacher, counselor, doctor, psychologist, all professions connected with humans animals and nature.

MIND/BODY

Greens are balanced, harmonious, and peaceful personalities. They need harmony in their life and prefer to live in a natural environment. They are the most balanced people in the color spectrum. They also have a powerful connection with nature. Living in the country, next to a forest or park or close to a lake or ocean is important for these friendly and heartfelt personalities. Greens are open, extroverted, expressive, friendly, communicative and heartfelt.

Greens perceive life through their heart. Their primary motivations are contentment and harmony. They judge their successes by how close they are to their friends or nature. Greens are content personalities. If they are in power and have found their place they need very little to be happy or feel needed. Their inner happiness and satisfaction is important to them and is fulfilled without much expectation. On one hand, Greens do not need to be first in competitions, wear the most expensive or beautiful clothing or express the ambition to have the best job in town. On the other hand they love the pleasures and advantages of luxury which comes as a direct result of success.

Greens want to feel happy and content with their lives. They understand clearly that the higher they set their goals the more difficult they will be to achieve. They also have an inner understanding of the natural cycles and laws of life. They believe that to live as a human being is life's most wonderful gift.

Green personalities are very talkative and communicative. They say exactly, what they think. They can talk for hours about almost any subject, often without saying very much. A good "chat" is therapeutic and allows them to release and express their deep feelings and concerns.

Greens have a need to talk about themselves and their problems so they can understand them and feel better. If they are unhappy or frustrated they will discharge their frustration verbally. It is difficult for Greens to hold back or contain their thoughts and feelings. They just come out naturally. If you are not familiar with a Greens behavior you might be offended or surprised at how direct and straightforward they are.

Greens are kinesthetic and have a strong connection with their physical bodies. For them, mind and body is one unit and all thoughts and emotions are quickly expressed physically. As an example, if they do not freely express their emotions they will feel uneasy, uncomfortable and in some cases become sick.

They have natural ways of expressing their emotions and feelings. Like animals who are in contact with nature, all emotional energies are expressed without reservation or holding back. If a Green is angry they will shout. If they are sad, tears will come. If they are jealous, you will see the reaction immediately. Greens don't think about their feelings, they live them.

Greens teach us that if we express our feelings and emotions naturally, the next step will be harmony and balance. If we hold back our feelings we will do nothing more than create unnecessary problems in our life. Unexpressed emotional energy will stay in our bodies and lower our life energy.

Many people have a feeling of low energy or powerlessness because they are afraid to naturally express their feelings. We communicate to the environment around us with our feelings and emotions. Greens understand this and live in natural harmony with mind and body.

Greens have a strong contact with both nature and their physical bodies. They have a need to express themselves and be physically active. Spending time in a garden, digging in the dirt or working with animals creates a special feeling for them. Animals, especially horses, cats and dogs, feel the Greens openness and natural understanding and are drawn to them.

In balance Greens have a strong connection with nature and physical reality. It is more than natural to them to deal with the material world, wealth and luxury. Greens have a balanced attitude towards prosperity. Every human being should live in an abundant environment. There is no need to suffer or live in poverty. They are also good in managing their own material possessions.

Greens have a definite connection with nature and mother earth and also have the ability to change and easily adjust themselves to different environments. They clearly understand the concept of change, a process that occurs in nature every day. They are not as easy going and fun oriented as Yellows but this is still an important issue for them. They have a tendency of taking life easy and enjoy most life situations the same as Yellows. However, they need more security and safety and their minds are much more analytical.

Green personalities are quick, abstract and analytical thinkers and can jump from one step to another without being concerned about the steps between. They prefer to develop and express their ideas and then to organize and delegate work. They are organized, efficient and have a need to understand everything they do. They process data both quickly and mentally and are able to make maximum use of this ability. Their knack of being able to communicate quickly is an expression of their flexible mind.

Greens are able to quickly recognize patterns and solutions to problems. They enjoy setting goals, which they want to achieve as soon as possible. They also enjoy mental stimulation but often don't have enough power or ambition to work hard and see those same goals to fruition. They prefer organizing, structuring, planing and especially communicating about their projects to actual hard, physical work.

Greens have high expectations and specific beliefs about life. This is especially prevalent in their relationships with other people and their own financial situation. They expect life to go their way. Contrary to most Deep-Green personalities, Greens are not very ambitious or hardworking people. They prefer a natural and easy going life rather than one which is hectic and filled with stress, based primarily on earning money and achieving goals.

They need to be independent and free in the sense that they have their own agenda and way of life. Greens need to feel, at least to themselves, that they are their own boss and are free to express, explore and change any situation.

Out of power Greens can be lethargic, irresponsible, stuck and resistant to change. Growth and change represent too much action and effort. With this attitude they cannot discover their true love of nature and may go through life without any direction or goals. With this as a basis, life has no meaning for them. They adjust to the status quo and adapt to their environment. Finding goals will be difficult because they have no strong ambitions. They occasionally question their purpose in life without finding answers or solutions.

Out of balance Greens often project their need to communicate and their love towards nature and animals. They prefer to be with their animals or alone with nature to experience a feeling of balance and communion. They often behave this way because they are afraid to confront themselves with an even greater adventure: to love, to communicate and to interact with other human beings with all their positive and negative tendencies. Personal growth, evolution and natural change are difficult to perceive for Greens who are out-of-power.

Greens can become passive and unoriented at times. They express similarities to cats, enjoying doing nothing at all for long periods of time. They just stretch out and relax, which allows them to create harmony and balance and to recharge their life energy batteries.

Unbalanced Greens are afraid to confront situations or problems. They prefer to stay on the outside, which creates their reputation of being superficial or shallow. They are afraid to open their hearts and experience the power of love and affection. They need to understand that learning only takes place by confronting and dealing with life situations or problems. If they never leave the warm "nest", or take any chances with their life, growth and change will never be possible.

Greens need to connect with their general love toward life. When they do they will discover goals for themselves which make life worth living. Also, when this occurs, they will take the necessary actions to make their own changes or allow the natural changes to take place by themselves.

In power Greens know that life, by itself, is enough. Spirituality means nature, balance and harmony. Being in contact with fellow human beings and nature is being in contact with God. Friendship, love and understanding are important aspects to a Greens sense of applied spirituality. The more friends you have, the more you can consider yourself as a spiritual or enlightened being.

SOCIAL LIFE

Greens are social and love to be with their family, relatives or friends. They love the secure feeling of being around family. To feel understood and accepted is very important to them.

Green personalities need harmony and prefer a relaxed, balanced, peaceful environment. Being around people allows them to communicate and express their deepest feelings. In addition, having contact with animals and nature is extremely fulfilling to these loving personalities.

Greens can talk for hours. It is therapeutic for them. They tend to talk about their own experiences much more than about other peoples concerns. They also have no fear of communicating with strangers without knowing them. These expressive personalities are often found in social groups or organizations. Community work and sharing life with their family and close friends is very rewarding to them.

Greens have a need to be with people, animals or nature. This interaction tells them they are alive and gives them the feeling of being needed and being part of nature. Because of their ability to share and communicate, Greens are often found in teaching or therapeutic professions.

RELATIONSHIPS AND INTIMACY

Green means relationships and interaction with humans, animals and nature. These relationships are their primary way of perceiving life. They view their world in terms of relating and personal interaction. Greens talk a lot about relationships: Who is going out with whom, why do you like him, is this the right partner for him or her? They need people to talk with and to share their thoughts and feelings. Green personalities are natural in their interactions with others.

They will talk with anyone without holding back or offering any resistance. It is natural for them to share their most intimate thoughts and feelings. They are open and forthcoming to the point where some people perceive them as insensitive or overwhelming.

On the other hand, often it is difficult for them to develop deep relationships. Shallow conversation and a general sense of openness does not necessarily guarantee a deep interpersonal connection or meaningful friendship. However, if they are willing to give and support others they can relate with almost every personality type. Greens just love to be together with their family or close friends.

Greens enjoy being sexually active. For them sex means aliveness, love and affection. In power Greens have a natural attitude towards sex and relationships because they understand the concepts of love and partnership. Greens match easily with Deep-Greens, Violets and all physical colors. A Deep-Reds security and groundedness is sought after, and a Reds power ads to the Greens mental and expressive abilities. Yellow personalities have a lightness which Greens love.

Greens need to understand a Blues loving and emotional way of life. Lavenders and Greens can talk about every subject for hours. As long as Green people can communicate and express themselves with their partners and they feel accepted and recognized, harmonious relationships are easy to achieve.

CAREER AND FINANCES

Greens have similar personality traits like Deep-Greens. Their financial attention is not on making money or achieving goals, but on having money and living a prosperous life. Greens are not fond of working very hard whether physically or mentally. They are also not completely responsible when it comes to earning money for themselves. They often find it easier to have someone else support them, or just decide to slow down and only earn enough money for their own basic needs. On the other hand, Greens are security conscious. They need to live in a safe and balanced environment where money and problems don't take up much space. Fighting for survival causes tension, something, which bothers Greens very much.

Greens are friendly and helpful. Because they know how to communicate what they want or need, they regularly receive help from others. They seem to understand the concept of nature's support and growth system. If you ask, you will receive. Because of their connection to the natural support system they often forget that it is also necessary to initiate action and to make things happen.

Greens solve their problems not only because they have friends or know the right people to fix things, but also because they have good analytical, organizing and planing abilities. The Greens strong mind/body connection and their willingness to take action allow them to solve problems efficiently and quickly.

Greens come up with detailed and clever ideas. They possess a natural intuition, which allows them to be quick-minded and innovative. But Greens normally do not act on their ideas for themselves. They will only take physical action and make their ideas or plans happen if they absolutely have to.

They often wait for others to show up, accept their ideas and then create them into physical reality. In most cases they do not have the ambition or stamina to create and finish their own ideas and plans.

Greens love to work with nature, animals or other people. They have an inner need to communicate in any form with their environment. They also need a friendly and balanced place in which to work. As a result of not being very ambitious or goal driven, their interests are more focused on nature and human, interpersonal issues.

Typical "green" occupations would include: Gardener, environmental researcher, farmer, social worker, animal caretaker, mother, teacher, therapist, counselor, secretary.

HEALTH, WELL-BEING AND GROWTH

The best method for Greens to find harmony is to accept full responsibility and live their own life to the best of their abilities. They need to get in contact with their own mind/body and see the natural flow of growth and love. If they know what they want and have defined their goals clearly, they will be supported by nature with unlimited energy.

Greens are natural healers and communicators and need to understand their purpose in life. They can bridge and unify mind and body and show humanity that friendship, sympathy, openness, communication and heartfulness are important aspects and qualities of human life. The moment Greens allow their body/mind to act naturally they have no difficulty in recharging their own batteries. In power Greens are healthy individuals. Their mind/body tells them or shows them exactly what to do to regain health in nearly any situation.

Living in a balanced, harmonious environment, close to nature, is therapeutic to them. Greens need to talk and express their feelings and thoughts to stay well and centered. They will be unhappy if they are taught to suppress their feelings and emotions. The biggest gift Greens can give themselves is to be a natural, pure and simple human being. Conversely, this is also the largest lesson they can teach and offer humanity.

Greens also need a lot of time for themselves. Relaxing at a peaceful lake, in a wonderful garden or in their own home is very recharging and fills their life energy batteries. Where other color personalities need little or no time to recharge their batteries, Green love to just be with close friends, talk about old times, take it easy, relax and enjoy life.

Greens usually need to be physically active. They prefer skiing, swimming, jogging with their dog, dancing and other activities, which bring them in contact with their mind/body and with nature. As long as Greens have no fear of changing and growing Mother Nature will support them. Growth is the most natural thing on earth as well as the entire universe.

DEEP-GREEN PERSONALITIES

The following are the qualities and action words associated with DEEP-GREEN personalities:

Area	Description
Physical	Material, physical, wealth, luxury, firmness, clarity of presentation and communication, structure, autocratic, resistance to change.
Emotional	Self-esteem, self-assertiveness, constancy, perseverance, tenacity, self-control, proud, superiority, idealized picture of oneself.
Mental	Quick minded, organized, communicative, ambitious, intelligent, accurate memory, high "I" value and expectations.
Spiritual	Mental concept and understanding of God.
Motivation	Achieving goals, being accepted and important, making money.
Mission/ Vision	Intellectual growth, to learn, express and teach others.
Growth	Acceptance, take responsibility for their actions, organize life.
Exercise	Walking, gym, aerobics, professional sports
Recharge battery	Nature, aerobics, sports, communication, mental and emotional balance.
Communication	Fast, direct, personal, precise, ideal communicators and teachers.
Interaction	Powerful, direct, verbal, intelligent, constant mental stimulation.
Relationships	High expectations, goal oriented, look for acceptance and understanding.
Social, Friends	Aristocratic, expensive life style, business friends, social events.
Sex, Intimacy	Attractive, need acceptance and security emotionally careful.

Money	Means luxury, wealth, superior powers, independence from others.
Success	Amount of money they earn, being accepted, achieving their goals.
Occupation	Workaholics, organizer, planers, boss, independent, financial promising careers, ideal for higher management positions.
Career	Bankers, entrepreneurs, lawyers, real estate or stock market broker, financial consultants, producers.

MIND/BODY

Deep-Green personalities are bright, intelligent and vigorous. They are communicative, organized, ambitious and love to surround themselves with people, nature and material wealth and luxury. They express the belief that every human being should live in prosperity and abundance. Their balance and harmony with nature is reflected in their ability to organize and handle material substances and wealth. To live in contact with nature means to live in prosperity and experience life to its fullest. Green personalities represent mind/body balance.

Deep-Greens integrate almost all the qualities of Green personalities. The primary difference is they are more intense and direct in everything they do. Deep-Greens are communicators like Greens but do so with more power and intensity. All Green personalities are mental and quick-minded, but Deep-Greens are extremely fast in their thinking, more detailed and more dynamic.

They also possess the ambition to achieve their goals. Greens love to be with nature, Deep Greens love to deal with nature and material items. Both color personalities are social but Deep-Greens tend to focus more on business and other social events that help them in their growth.

Deep-Greens love to be around people because they need the constant interaction and stimulation. Talking with friends or business associates and sharing ideas and thoughts is as refreshing and recharging as taking a shower. They need the friction, which is created by human interaction. They also know how to express themselves. In addition, they are excellent communicators and know how to impress others.

Deep-Greens love to give advice and to tell other people what to do. They think they know everything better and this is often the case. They are the perfect teachers and communicators. Their powerful, fast and precise communication allows them to express their ideas with strength and clarity. Most of the time they say exactly what they think.

Deep-Greens have the ability to quickly make the point in a conversation. While other life colors might need ten minutes or more to explain a situation or concept, Deep-Greens can say it in a few sentences. On the other hand, if they are unhappy or frustrated they will discharge and verbally let go of their frustration. Their verbal attacks can often cut deeply into other people's hearts. It is difficult to win an argument against a Deep-Green personality.

Deep-Green need to constantly stimulate themselves or be stimulated by others. They are easily bored. It is difficult for them to perceive a moment of mental relaxation or emptiness of mind. Their mind works too fast and is too active to let go and relax. They love communicating with others, talking, watching movies or reading an exciting book as a means of relaxation and recharging their batteries.

Deep-Greens are ambitious and want to achieve their own goals. They perceive life through their quick and competitive minds. The highest goals they can set for themselves are how productive and perfect they can be in their work and life. After they achieve their goals they feel wonderful. For them, life can be viewed as a large "to do" list. Having these specific goals and ambitions make their life very special. On the other hand, after they achieve their goals they sometimes feel a certain sense of emptiness.

Deep-Greens exhibit perseverance, tenacity, firmness and consistency. These strong and self-asserted personalities are often afraid of change because they have precise and specific viewpoints and opinions.

Because they are quick-minded and have extremely strong will power, they need to be independent and go their own way. They don't like taking orders from other people because they think of themselves as more clever and intelligent. They *know* they can do it better. Deep-Greens are self-conscious and have a superior feeling towards others.

Deep-Green personalities are perfectionists. They have high expectations toward themselves and toward others. They set the highest goals for themselves and until they are achieved, will not feel a sense of satisfaction. The high expectations they place on their friends or co-workers can create a considerable amount of pressure. It is extremely difficult to fulfill a Deep-Greens ideals and expectations. Even if you do they would still think it could have done better. Deep-Greens need to understand those unusually high expectations can sometimes be the cause of unhappiness and frustration. Setting goals is important for Deep-Greens, but the less they expect, the more fulfilled their life will be.

Deep-Green personalities are quick, abstract, analytical thinkers and can easily jump from one step to the next. In contrast to Yellow-Browns, they don't like to deal with the detailed steps between. They prefer developing ideas, organizing plans and delegating work to others for execution. These quick-thinkers are organized, efficient and have a need to understand everything they do.

They recognize patterns and solutions to problems quickly and love to set goals, which they can achieve within a short period of time. Deep-Greens are ambitious, competitive and enjoy the challenges connected with specific tasks at hand. They prefer organizing, structuring and planing to hard, physical work. They are willing to spend their time on the mental processes and then pay others to do the real, physical labor.

Out of power Deep-Greens are afraid of personal failure and the lack of recognition. They try to compensate this concern by being in control of every aspect of their life and showing a self-controlled superiority and proudness. Their autocratic temperament and wish to impress is grounded in their need to have a strong self-esteem and a high "I" value.

Deep-Greens need to be mentally in control of their own life. If they find themselves in a situation in which they are not in control they become frustrated, fearful and stressed. They must learn to let go and understand that not every aspect of life can be controlled by human efforts. One of life's biggest lessons for them is to enjoy the process of life itself and have fun with what they do.

Deep-Greens can become embittered, frustrated and aggravated if they repress their power, do not achieve their goals and ambitions, or are not in control of their life. If this occurs it is difficult to be around them.

They are aggressive, impatient and judgmental. They have a tendency of being controlling and rigid in their viewpoints and behavior and can insult and hurt others easily. If they want something they want it immediately.

These perfectionists project their high expectations and often blame others for their own problems and disappointments.

The life purpose of Deep-Green personalities is to enjoy and experience life with an open heart, to grow intellectually, and to learn and to live as an example for others. Deep-Greens are hungry for knowledge and always want to be mentally stimulated.

Spirituality is not an unfamiliar concept for Deep Greens. Because they are very mental and quick minded they are able to understand and teach what God or religion is all about. They are quick in processing spiritual concepts from a mental standpoint but have difficulty in perceiving a real experience and connection with the inner source.

SOCIAL LIFE

In our society, Deep-Green is associated with money, wealth and luxury. The aristocratic Deep-Greens usually live an expensive life style and need money around them. Money and an exclusive life style are important. Material wealth shows their high social status and gives them security. They can do nearly anything if they are paid well for their services. Deep-Green also relates to conservative beliefs and social behavior.

It is not uncommon for Deep-Greens to have strikingly pretty features. They pay a great deal of attention to their physical appearance and prefer wearing modern, expensive and/or sexy clothes. These proud personalities might show up at a business meeting or go to the theater driving a deep-green BMW, wearing an Armani suit or dress, and decked out with expensive jewelry.

Sometimes Deep-Greens have difficulty in accepting all human beings as equal. They have an attitude of superiority and normally only mix with people of their own strata. Learning to understand other people's behavior and attitudes is a major task for them.

Deep-Greens are powerful communicators and know how to express themselves. They are social personalities who know exactly what they want and desire.

RELATIONSHIPS AND INTIMACY

One of the largest challenges facing Deep-Green personalities is that of relationships. They want close, intimate and loving relationships with acceptance, warmth and support. Deep-Greens have unusually high expectations toward others which most of the time cannot be fulfilled. They usually look to others for qualities they are missing and find that no one can deliver those qualities except themselves.

Deep-Green personalities normally experience difficulties in finding a partner they can completely accept. They can always find something wrong or not quite adequate.

They easily grow out of partnerships and become bored quickly if their partner is not equally ambitious, goal-oriented and lives up to their expectations. Communicating with their partner is essential for Deep-Greens. Discussing ideas and the projects they are working on is an important part of interacting with their partners and people in general.

Deep-Greens are usually both physically and mentally attractive. Their royal behavior opens many doors for them, privately as well as in business. Sex is not a primary issue but can represent a deep, intimate physical and emotional experience. However, they can be sexual without getting involved with strong feelings. They can close down mentally or distinguish between close intimacy and pure physical enjoyment.

Deep-Greens are impressed by a Violets visionary ideas and charismatic power. Reds, on the other hand, stimulate them through their physical power. Orange and Deep-Green personalities need a lot of space to themselves.

Blues and Indigos seem to be too emotional and introverted to create a good match. Deep-Greens understand the way of thinking of Deep-Reds and Yellow-Browns. Greens and Deep-Greens have a lot in common yet the ambition to achieve goals needs to be there. Deep-Greens need to understand the Yellows playfulness to create harmonious relationships.

Deep-Greens need strong and equally intelligent partners who they can accept and appreciate. Once they finally do open up they can become very close to their partners. A common reason for marriage is because it normally guarantees financial security and a high social status.

Deep Greens are definitely on the lookout for unmarried royalty. And why not? Wouldn't anyone want to marry a king or a princess?

CAREER AND FINANCES

Deep-Greens are good at organizing and coordinating projects or teams. They often own their own businesses or can be found in independent and high level positions. Their openness, strong mental capacities, communication skills and intelligence, enhance their ability to achieve leadership positions and allows them the feeling of a sense of importance and recognition. These career conscious personalities and successful entrepreneurs are textbook examples of typical workaholics.

Deep-Greens come up with solutions to problems quickly and efficiently. This is a result of their clear, quick thinking, seeing new options and their powerful communicative skills. Deep-Greens are adept at organizing and planing and know how to clearly communicate their ideas and concepts. This gives them the tremendous advantage of being able to solve their own as well as other people's problems. They consider most problems as tests to be solved because they are so ambitious and goal oriented. Quicker and better solutions to any problems bring Deep-Greens the most satisfaction.

Deep-Green personalities are helpful and generous to others with reference to tips and advice. They have the ability and capacity to help others with solving their problems. However, taking action and physically helping out is not their strongest trait. They can become frustrated and disinterested if their advice is not followed. They do not understand why other people do not adhere to and act on their advice.

For Deep-Greens to access their full power and live up to their full potential in the world of business they prefer being self-employed, independent, owning their own businesses or being responsible in top positions.

They like to delegate authority. They can be found in many areas as long as their job is well paying, stimulating and highly respected. Deep- Greens love money and what it can do for them. They are drawn to occupations, which have to do with money and will guarantee them high income.

Typical "Deep-Green" occupations are: Bankers, entrepreneurs, lawyers, marketing experts, real estate or stock market brokers, sales persons for expensive items, executives, producers and financial consultants

HEALTH, WELL-BEING AND GROWTH

The best method for Deep-Greens to find harmony is to stay emotionally and mentally centered and to take full responsibility for their own life. By recognizing what they truly want and then taking active steps they take control over their life and can live their full dynamic power.

Being aware of their strong intellect and high expectations will guide them toward more mental relaxation, patience and heartfulness. They need to channel their strong and intense mental-expressive energies into a positive direction. The more Deep-Greens feel and connect with their heart, the more content and successful they will be.

Deep-Greens are not very interested in purely physical activities. To exercise or practice any sport for fun makes little or no sense to them. They will become active if they establish a good reason to stay physically fit. These would include such logical things as health, a good figure or overall attractiveness. Physical exercise is more than just for health or recharging. It also provides an opportunity for calming the mind from its constant need for stimulation and activity.

Deep-Green personalities need to actively work on mental relaxation and focus. Autogenic training, mental relaxation tapes, visualization, dream journeys and brain machines are proven methods to achieve a deeper and more relaxed state of mind. Once the mind is calm, they open up and are able to move into higher dimensions.

Even if Deep-Greens appear to be strong willed, powerful and independent, deep inside they harbor the fear of not being equal, accepted or recognized. The biggest lesson for them is to accept this insecurity which is simply a part of life. Life itself cannot be controlled.

Life is change, growth and expansion and this insecurity can be one of the treasures life has to offer. The only constant in life is change. To understand this fact creates flexibility and acceptance

Deep-Greens must learn to recharge their life energy batteries on a regular basis. Once they are able to relax their mind and let go of their high expectations they will find enough inner peace to allow relaxation and recharging to occur.

BLUE PERSONALITIES

The following are the qualities and action words associated with Blue personalities:

Area	Description
Physical	Helpful, caring, peaceful, relaxation and recuperation, tranquillity, calm physical activity, physical relaxation or tiredness.
Emotional	Heartfelt, sensitive, caring, nurturing, calm, deep feelings, peace plus gratification, tenderness, love, dedication, empathy, trust, surrender, easily hurt, self-pity.
Mental	Clarity, calm, peaceful, balanced thinking, contentment, quiet.
Spiritual	God is love and compassion, relationships and spirituality are most important.
Motivation	Peace and harmony they experience how much support and love they can give.
Mission/ Vision	To serve mankind, give and receive love and compassion.
Growth	Change victim/helpless state of mind into responsibility/in charge state of mind, taking care of themselves, stay clear.
Exercise	Walking, bicycling, picnicking, all water activities, beach, swimming.
Recharge battery	Meditation, soft music, walking in nature, live in a nurturing, sensitive environment.
Communication	Soft voices, feelings are expressed, personal and intimate.
Interaction	Conservative, family oriented, careful and supportive.
Relationships	Harmonious, peaceful, loving, caring relationships are essential.
Social, Friends	Very social, do anything for family and friends.

Sex, Intimacy	Sensitivity and love, need intimacy more then sex.
Money	Security, safety, satisfy needs.
Success	How much they give love and how much they are loved by others.
Occupation	All caring, supportive occupations, wherever help is needed.
Career	Nurse, caretaker, priest, housewife, childcare, social worker, teacher, therapist, consultant, healer, secretary, accountant.

MIND/BODY

Blues are the most caring, nurturing and protective personalities in the color-spectrum. They live out of their hearts and their emotions. Their life purpose is to serve, help and love others. They teach humanity that without love nothing else matters. Blues are on this planet to serve mankind.

The honest Blue personality represents surrender, devotion, dedication, tradition and lasting values. Blues are introverted, friendly, loving and heartfelt.

A Blues motivation is to serve and help other people to receive love, attention and affection. They process ideas and concepts more on their feelings and intuitions than they do from a mental standpoint. As a result, Blues do not feel comfortable when highly intellectual subjects are being discussed.

In today's society, intuition and emotional behavior are not accepted as much as intellectual thinking or the discussion of facts. But for Blues, there are no real facts. They have a tendency of operating and reacting much more from their feelings and intuitions.

Blues have an inner knowledge and wisdom and they feel and know what is right without needing facts or data for substantiation. The moment they become quiet inside, they will recognize or hear an inner voice or guidance, which will tell them what to do. They can easily tune into other people and feel precisely what is going on.

Blues are the most emotional of all the color personalities. They often feel lost if they don't have the opportunity to clear their way through their intense jungle of deep feelings. Helpful activities for Blues would include talking with friends about their inner life, writing a journal or just being quiet so their intense emotions can calm down.

Blues are more concerned about others then they are about themselves They are born caretakers and mothers. They remember other people's birthdays, are concerned about the sick and have always a shoulder for others to cry on. They are born advisers, counselors, caretakers and nurses. Many people enjoy being with Blues because they transmit love, acceptance and forgiveness.

Blues cry easily and primarily release their emotions, joy, sorrow, sadness and happiness, through tears. The other color personalities often have problems understanding the Blues intense emotionality. However, this emotional depth gives them the ability to be warm, sympathetic and protective.

Blues major gifts are their ability to give "unrestricted love", their intuition, and their "inner knowledge." No matter what happens, Blues will always forgive. They are often seen as "too nice" and therefore are regularly taken advantage of.

Blues accept other people's authority without offering any resistance. They take commands and orders easily and are willing to do anything to follow directions, which are given. It is no wonder that people regularly take advantage of Blues. As a result of this attitude and belief, they often find themselves in helpless situations. Blues often make statements like: "I am not in charge of the situation.", "What can I do?", or "I feel helpless". They need to come to the understanding that they are their own authority.

Blues are primarily focused on other peoples concerns. They enjoy listening to others problems and have the capacity to understand and accept whatever other people might be going through. Because they spend so much time with other people's problems they sometimes forget to look at their own. The most important issue for Blues is to spend more time working on their own personal growth.

The biggest challenge for any Blue person is to just say, "NO!" They have a basic fear that others might push them back, reject them or no longer love them. The fear of hurting other people's feelings reflects and mirrors their own fears of being hurt. They need to recognize the enormous benefits of Self-Love and also to understand that "no" does not mean the same as, " I don't love you." They need to find their boundaries and borders with other people because they have a tendency of allowing friends and even strangers to come into their energy field without having adequate protection.

Sometimes Blues even take on other people's energies and qualities. This can especially happen while they are helping or nurturing others in the capacity of nurses or caretakers. This can occur to the point where they actually take on other people's sicknesses or problems.

They need to recognize and accept that they are loved. Because of their sensitivity and their deep feelings they can easily be hurt. They want to feel loved and accepted and will often do anything to receive a small amount of attention or affection.

Blues are precise and clear in their thinking. From a mental standpoint they are usually in a peaceful and calm state of mind. They focus more on their feelings and emotions than on their thoughts. They feel their own and other peoples thoughts. On the other hand it is difficult for then to formulate their perceptions into detailed, analytical language.

Blues do not like physical activity or work. For theses sensitive beings the physical world often seems loud, brutal and harsh. They prefer to reside in their own emotional world.

They enjoy sports they can practice with friends and family. These would include such activities as walking, swimming and simple ball games. Because they are not very physically active, and because Blue is the color of expansion and wideness, they can easily gain weight.

If Blues are not living in harmony they can be dramatic and consuming, always looking for someone to love. They see themselves as victims and can be manipulative and filled with self-pity. They live out of the belief: "I need to give love in order to feel worthy and be loved in return." Blue personalities might regularly make statements such as: "If he really loves me, then he..." or, "He won't forget my birthday because I never forget his." or, "Why is he doing this to me?"

Out of power Blues think life seems to treat them badly and that they are victims of certain circumstances. They live a life filled with depression, seeing themselves as martyrs, consumed with self-pity. Through their lack of self-confidence and feelings of worthlessness they often question if they are truly and honestly loved. If they are told they are loved a hundred-times and only criticized for something one time, they will remember the criticism for years.

Unbalanced Blues consider themselves responsible for every mistake ever made in the history of the universe. They take all matters personally and excuse themselves a thousand times, even if they have not been involved.

In additional to being good helpers, givers and teachers, Blues are very spiritual personalities. They believe in a God, a higher power in the universe. God and religion play an important role in their life. They could not exist without spirituality and a believe that there is a higher purpose in life. It is extremely important for Blues to live a good, affectionate and spiritual life. Spirituality means living day-by-day with this inner guidance and intuition which connects Blues to truth and love. They have tremendous faith, belief and trust in God. In bad times they are able to connect with their powerful inner source so they can continue to help and support others. They love to visit churches or other spiritual power spots to recharge their inner battery.

SOCIAL LIFE

Blues enjoy being around people all the time. They are very social, the perfect caretakers and helpers, always interested in and concerned about other peoples needs. These traits allow them to be loving and in service to their family or friends. Blues are found in all areas of society, wherever service and support is needed.

The biggest gift for these loving personalities is to help and support their family and friends. They are family oriented people who love being with their partners, children or friends. Planing picnics, creating nice meals, nothing seems too much if it is enjoyed and appreciated. Blues have friends for life. Once they really like someone they won't forget them, even if they don't have close personal contact anymore. They will write letters, send birthday cards or think about other reasons to communicate their love and appreciation.

Blues represent the female or mother figure in our society. Unfortunately, this aspect is often not as appreciated as the male, productive, active portion. As long as Blues are appreciated and loved they are willing to be in service to help and nurture others.

RELATIONSHIPS AND INTIMACY

The most important aspect of a Blues life is living in healthy, harmonious relationships. Blues want to be loved and appreciated. They make wonderful mates because they love to take care of and support their loved ones. They will do anything to create a happy and harmonious family life. They often expect their partner to return their love or be as much supportive and caring. They need to understand that other color personality characters might not understand the strong emotional depth they possess and also have different emotional and mental behaviors.

Blues want to be married and live in affectionate, solid family units. Love and affection is more important to them than sex and passion. Kissing, cuddling and feeling their partner's affection and emotional love are more important than sexual excitement and stimulation. Sexuality is a deep, emotional and spiritual experience and creates a strong bond between the lovers.

Blues are loyal and monogamous. They need to be aware that if they are too emotionally demanding with their partner, they might push them away. In disharmonious relationships they have problems letting go. The very words, "let go," are key words for all Blues. Blues love the Deep-Reds strength, the Yellow Browns security and the Deep-Greens independence. But they need to make sure they are not being used and that their relationships are based on sensitivity and love.

Oranges and Blues are the opposite side of the spectrum and therefore can learn tremendously from each other. Blues relating with Blues can be too emotional where none of them has the power to lead and inspire. Blues love the passion and spirituality of Violets and Lavenders. Whites and Blues have God and spirituality as a basis for good relationships.

The two most important goals of Blue personalities are spirituality and relationships. If both aspects are in balance they will live a peaceful, happy and content life.

CAREER AND FINANCES

Blue personalities are not very interested in money. Emotional and spiritual values are far more important and play a much larger role in their life. They are careful with money and have a rather conservative approach to it. They need to make sure to cover all their expenses and needs and normally do not take any financial risks.

Blues are born nurses, caretakers, counselors and therapists. They are also born listeners and easily tune into other people's feelings and thoughts.

If Blues choose an occupation, which does not offer these opportunities, they are still usually known as the "nice, good person around the corner." They would be the people you go to if you have any problems or want to unload any emotional disturbances.

In the past Blues have mainly been found in private or social occupations or in their homes as mothers or housewives. In the last few decades more opportunities have become available and Blues began to expand their business ideas and careers. They are not very ambitious but they are loyal, supportive and team oriented. They lead by both their team spirit and by example.

They show others that working together and creating a supportive environment allows a team to achieve much better results. "The whole is more, then the sum of its parts," makes perfect sense to Blue personalities.

Blues solve their problems by being peaceful, looking inside themselves, and asking the right questions. They must learn to listen and trust their intuition, their inner voice, and then deal with the situation. Because of their strong intuition and their inner knowledge, Blues usually know what they should do. Their main problem is taking action and making changes. The biggest challenge for Blues is letting go of old habits and patterns and openly embracing new situations.

Blues need some time to make decisions. They are not as quick and sharp as Greens or as detailed as Yellow-Browns. But through their intuition they are able to make valid and long lasting decision which are not only valuable for themselves, but also for the whole of a group or society. The moment Blues listen to their intuitions and take action they will make tremendous growth and will expand their loving and nurturing life energy to serve mankind.

Blues are good listeners and have the ability to tune into other people's inner world. They have a strong intuition and healing power. This is why they are often found in professions in which they can be helpful, nurturing or supportive.

Typical "Blue" occupations are: Nurse, caretaker, priest, nun, housewife, mother, child care worker, service personal, social-worker, counselor, teacher, therapist, consultant, healer, secretary, accountant, personal manager and volunteer.

HEALTH, WELL-BEING AND GROWTH

To become centered, Blues must learn the difficult lesson of loving themselves. If they can overcome their biggest fear, which is to not be loved and to be alone, they can express their deep feelings freely and then live a compassionate, happy and fulfilling life.

It is important for Blues to set their own boundaries and make clear decisions. They must learn to say, "No," if it feels like "no." Connecting with their personal power and then using it allows them to achieve their goals and give out even more love.

Blues need to create their own peaceful and harmonious environment. They need to make an active and willful decision as to what people they want to have as friends and what private and work environments they will accept.

Blues need a lot of time for themselves. They like being in a quiet atmosphere, listening to harmonious music or just sitting in a peaceful room. Being alone is relaxing and allows them to go within. Allowing peace and silence to occur are important activities for Blues to find their purpose in life.

Meditation and prayer are the most important and powerful tools they can use to achieve inner peace and happiness and to recharge their own life energy batteries. Going to church or a meditation class is an excellent way of meeting like-minded people and getting involved into a spiritual way of life.

Blues need to constantly be aware of their sensitive and powerful emotional system. Understanding their Mind/Body relationship will help them to stay healthy and strong.

If Blues have a question or want to solve a problem, they need to be quiet, stay centered and go inward. If they ask a question in this peaceful state of mind they will hear and immediately sense the answer inside. The challenge for Blues is not only to hear and trust their inner voice, but also to act on it and live their inner knowledge in the real world.

INDIGO PERSONALITIES

The following are the qualities and action words associated with INDIGO personalities:

Area	Description
Physical	Deep inner feelings, sensitivity, integrity, meditative awareness, introverted, androgynous, authenticity.
Emotional	Universal love, sensitivity, depth of feelings, inner communication, trust, loyalty, honest surrender, devotion, innocence.
Mental	Aware, bright, artistic, clarity, creative and independent, intuition, inner knowing, higher mind, dedication.
Spiritual	Higher knowledge, truth, spiritual, universal love, awareness and consciousness, experience inner planes of existence.
Motivation	Follow their higher truth and love and their inner guidance.
Mission/ Vision	Spiritual growth, love and service, express their inner knowing.
Growth	Inner awareness, intuitive changes, guided by their heart-intuition.
Exercise	Walking, dancing, swimming, meditative, spiritual exercises.
Recharge battery	Meditation, music, create own space, connect with God-Inner Self.
Communication	Soft, female voice with feeling, intuitive and inner communication.
Interaction	Considerate, careful, sensitive and divine action.
Relationships	Caring, depth, heartfelt, soul-to-soul, spiritual connections.
Social, Friends	Follow inner rules, not societies, few close friends.

Sex, Intimacy	Deep, divine experience, careful, open up only to close partners.
Money	Clear concept, but unimportant, follow higher values and truth.
Success	Connection to God and Higher Self, live love and spirituality on earth.
Occupation	Helping others, live in harmony with their higher beliefs and truth.
Career	Spiritual healer, teacher, musician, artist, social worker, writer.

MIND/BODY

Indigo personalities experience life through their deep inner feelings. These calm and pleasant individuals are connected with their inner knowing, intuition or higher mind. Their life long search for higher truth and consciousness allows them to radiate an authenticity and clarity, which is not found in other color personalities.

Indigos have an inner need to express their spirituality or religiousness. They are considered to be very deep in their feelings and perceptions about life. They also seem to be born as conscious beings and as children know what they want and how to act. Indigos cannot be told what to do, think, feel or what the truth is. Their inner knowing and guidance gives them all the information they need. They just know the truth within.

An Indigo personality motivation is to experience life as a divine universal being with compassion and love. To them, life is like an endless ocean, filled with divine love and energy, full of unbelievable treasures. Indigos are content if they can express their feelings of spirituality, religiousness and love and know that the world around them is responding to their message.

Indigos have a high sense of honor and their own internal values and belief system. They cannot be told to live by others people's ideas, beliefs, standards or concepts. Their inner strength and power comes from their connection with God or Love. To them, universal Love is the connecting force in the universe.

Indigos know that all humans are divine beings. We are not only physical, emotional or mental beings, but are connected with a higher power, which we call God or Love. Indigos also know that everything in the universe is interconnected. There is no separation. This inner knowledge makes it even more difficult for them to understand why humans treat themselves and planet earth so badly.

Indigos are seen as the new leaders for the coming times. They seem to have an inherent understanding and awareness about human life and its universal implications. They don't need facts, statistics or data to be convinced that our planet is in a bad condition. They also don't need a reason to help humanity to grow spiritually. Their whole existence shows them we are powerful spiritual beings waking up from the dream of unconsciousness and darkness.

Centered Indigos have the energy and power to guide humanity into an age of awareness and true spirituality. In the past, Indigos were often found in religious groups or organizations. This was their only method of practicing spirituality and discovering God within. In our society it is no longer necessary to be part of limited religious groups or organizations. As a result, today's Indigo personalities have the freedom to live their inner feelings and their need to communicate with God without fear of repercussions.

Indigos often appear as soft, sensitive and even androgynous. They incorporate both male and female aspects within themselves. Because of their androgynous appearance and their advanced spirituality, other people sometimes tend to see them as introverted or in extreme cases as bizarre and eccentric

In power Indigos are aware, bright, creative and independent individuals with deep feelings and strong intuitions. They follow their inner knowing and abide by higher truths.

They understand that life should be treated with integrity, compassion and love. They also understand spiritual concepts far more easily then physical concepts. Indigos are more interested in learning about higher principal's then social beliefs or limited physical realities. No social pressures will force them to compromise or follow rules they do not agree with.

Indigos integrate their intelligence with a higher understanding, consciousness and awareness. They are aware and bright in their perceptions of humanity and the universe and are guided by their intuitions and inner knowledge. They seem to be born with an awareness of who they are and what their purpose in life is. Their insight and knowledge seems to come from a different source then our limited intellect.

Indigos have no particular need to understand the mental concept of an idea or situation. They don't process life through their intellect or their rational minds. They are clear and bright thinkers but perceive life more through intuition and feelings. They often come up with unorthodox, intuition-based concepts and views of a situation that might be unfamiliar to other color personalities.

Indigos have sensitive, physical bodies. For most of them, intense physical activity is much too harsh and disturbing. They prefer soft and balanced physical activities to intense exercises or competitive sports. Their favorite activities would include, taking a walk, jogging or meditative exercises. On the other hand, they have a need to express their creativity, which they often do through dancing, painting, writing or other artistic endeavors.

Because Indigos have a highly developed system, they are uncommonly sensitive and intuitive. They seem to be able to sense and detect energies, emotions and feelings or even spirits, auras and other dimensions. Their high vibration allows them to move into inner dimensions of existence. Indigos are considered to be closer to God than other personality colors. A more appropriate description might be that their "InnerNet" is higher developed and therefore more capable of receiving and connecting with higher realities.

With their clarity and innocence, Indigos are extremely truthful. They must live their life in accordance with the highest of principles. They know we are all divine beings within a greater plan. Life has meaning and we as humans are creating our own reality. While they are honest and independent, they are also very compassionate and accepting.

Indigos need a peaceful and harmonious environment whether at work or at home. Because of their sensitivity and their depth of feelings they need to create their own atmosphere of understanding and clarity.

If Indigos do not follow their own way they will become depressed, anxious and self-destructive. They can also become emotionally closed, introverted, withdrawn from friends and society and hide behind a large, "energetic-emotional" wall. Conservative, rigid thinking and the inability to express their deep feelings and their inner truth will cause them to feel sad and isolated.

If Indigos feel helpless, caught up in social rules, but don't want to compromise, they will withdraw from society, create emotional walls around themselves and reside within, without much contact with the outside world. Indigos can become withdrawn and introverted if they don't understand how to live their power and express their compassion and deep feelings of love.

Out of power Indigos can become frightened and disoriented. They lose touch with their inner knowing and feelings and then can't quite understand life anymore. They often turn to drugs and alcohol to hide from their confusion and quiet their inner voices.

The current state of the planet is not what they envision or understand and therefore they tend to be frustrated and confused. They are plagued with questions such as: "If we are one, if everything alive is interconnected, how can we be so brutal and violent to one other? How can humanity be so insensitive and unspiritual?"

When not in power, the sensitive Indigos, with their deep feelings, have problems adjusting to the world as it is right now. They feel isolated, misunderstood, as if they were from another planet. Their sensitive physical and emotional system causes them to withdraw.

Indigos need to connect with their deep feelings and their inner knowledge. If they trust their inner voice they will gain back their power and will understand that the universe - God is a part of them. They will understand life's larger plan, of which we are all a part.

SOCIAL LIFE

Society and Indigos are not a good match. In power Indigos do not follow societies rules or regulations. They have an inner knowing which they feel they have to follow. Indigos function on truth and spirituality, not on false ideals or political ambitions.

Their advanced spiritual thinking and behavior and their focus on truth and loyalty to their inner feelings make it difficult for them to adjust to societies rules. They have a tendency of withdrawing from society because they are often misunderstood.

In power Indigos have learned to live and function in society within their own, very private space. They find ways to express their inner desires and feelings into forms of creativity, which influence and lead people toward creating a better world. Indigos have few close friends. They know whom they can trust and they also know if they meet an old, ancient friend.

Out of power Indigos might adjust to society and negate or suppress their inner knowing and truth. They become introverted and hide behind a conservative, stiff and rigid attitude. Often Indigos live out their spirituality in religious groups or organizations. This gives them the opportunity to be with God and to express their inner needs.

Indigos are not very social. They are too sensitive and feel other people's pains and problems so much that they have to be careful in their interactions. They prefer to meet with people on a basis of spirituality and love.

RELATIONSHIPS AND INTIMACY

Indigos need mates who will be nurturing, dedicated and understanding while allowing them their independence and curiosity. They are careful in their selection of partners but once they have decided on their soul mate they will be loyal, faithful and monogamous.

Indigos need to be with partners who can understand their advanced, spiritual way of thinking. They are gentle and committed partners who are best friends and companions. Indigos generally integrate both female and male qualities and therefore often have androgynous appearances. Male Indigos, with their extremely sensitive bodies and nervous systems, often have female characteristics.

But Indigos are also great lovers. Once they feel safe and are off guard they can be passionate and full of deep love. Sex is a deeply spiritual experience where two beings of energy merge into cosmic oneness. Most in power Indigos do not have strong rules or regulations towards sexuality. Sexuality is not a male or female expression or a physical act, but a spiritual union of two beings.

Because Indigos incorporate both male and female qualities they often do not require relationships as we know them. Indigos love to be with Lavender, Violet or White personalities. They inspire and assure that other spiritual oriented people live on this planet.

All physical personality types seem to be too rude and brutal for a healthy loving relationship. Yellows and Indigos love to play and have fun together. The Green personalities can deal with the bright and clear mental abilities of Indigos.

Yellow-Browns and Deep-Reds also have a conservative approach toward life. But they usually do not understand the depth and love Indigos feel inside. As long as Indigos feel a deep inner connection with their partners they will be very loving and passionate mates.

CAREER AND FINANCES

Indigos are intellectual but they also incorporate awareness, brightness and sensitivity. Because they feel so much for others they are often willing to support and work with or for others. Indigo personalities are loyal. They would never lie, cheat or steal. Friends or employers can always count on them. This trustworthiness and friendliness often creates many opportunities.

Indigos solve their problems when they trust their inner senses. They will always receive the correct answer if they look inside themselves. They are happiest when they are able to live their lives in harmony with their beliefs and when they are able to help other souls on the planet. They feel successful when they know they are being aware and living the highest truth of which they are capable.

Indigos are often found in service, social or artistic occupations. They want to help and support society, but if they are in harmony with their inner knowing and in power, they know a higher task is waiting for them.

Indigos prefer occupations, which allow them the freedom to connect with life in its various forms. The work they do must be in harmony with their spiritual beliefs and perceptions of life. They have a need to love and be compassionate with their work. They enjoy jobs, which enable them to love and support others. Because they are closely connected to God and the Universal Life Energy, Indigos can be powerful spiritual healers, counselors and teachers.

Typical "Indigo" occupations are: Spiritual healer, teacher, musician, artist, nurse, mother, social worker, child caretaker, musician, writer, artist and designer.

HEALTH, WELL-BEING AND GROWTH

Indigos need to connect with their inner knowing, their deep feelings, and the higher mind. To stay in power, they have to feel and trust their inner voice. If they live out their inner beliefs and feelings they can create an environment which radiates peace, love and understanding.

Their bodies are usually very fragile. And, they are not used to the unbalanced and stressful environment, which dominates our planet. Their androgynous appearance, personality and beliefs do not fit into societies concepts of male, female, good bad, etc. As a result, they may have difficulty in adjusting to our unbalanced and insensitive environment.

Indigos need to create an environment which allows them to stay centered, peaceful and in contact with their inner knowing. The real world life is too loud, brutal and insensitive for these fragile personalities. If Indigos are in harmony they have no problems recharging their life energy batteries. They know that they are a part of this vast system of universal consciousness and energy. Whenever an Indigos mind/body is quiet and peaceful, they will connect with the universal energy flow. Indigos have the unique ability to recharge and heal themselves from the inside to the outside.

Indigos need to get in contact with their mission and their vision in life. They understand that life has a meaning and that they are part of a much larger entity called God. Meditation and prayer are important tools for Indigos to gain harmony, balance and strength. They will receive all the answers to all their questions if they simply ask their higher mind for inner guidance. They will create harmony by living their lives with awareness and inner power and expressing their beliefs in love and understanding.

Indigos need to step into the real world to show humanity what a wholistic society and spiritual life can look and be like. The most difficult yet most rewarding action they can undertake is standing up for their convictions and beliefs.

VIOLET PERSONALITIES

The following are the qualities and action words associated with VIOLET personalities:

Area	Description
Physical	Charisma, fascination, sensitive, physical activity, ideas made fact, innovative, futuristic, fusion of subject and object.
Emotional	Sensitive, mystical union, intimacy, passion fascination, visual, passion, guilt, aloof, freedom, unconventional, independent.
Mental	Visionary, magical, theoretical, intuitive, creative, innovative, visualizes trends and future, professional-scientific nature.
Spiritual	Magical and mystical union, transformation, cosmic flow, universal perception of God, unity of earth and spirit.
Motivation	Live their vision and fulfill their destiny, need to reach big audience.
Mission/ Vision	Lead and inspire humanity, realize and express visionary ideas.
Growth	Magical transformation, expansion.
Exercise	Activities combining physical and mental skills, like tennis.
Recharge battery	Music, meditation, mind/body technique, male/female integration.
Communication	Universal, global, impersonal, charismatic, magnetic, passionate and powerful, direct.
Interaction	Passionate, direct, theoretical.
Relationships	Committed, demanding, focused, share vision, travel and inspiration.
Social, Friends	Anti-social, humanitarians, planetary and universal, inspire and motivate society.
Sex, Intimacy	Passionate, strong sexual drive, mystical, tantric male-female union.

Money	Power, influence, possibilities, new projects, fulfill creative ideas.
Success	Live vision, how many people they reach, teach and transform.
Occupation	Creative, innovative and independent, express visionary ideas.
Career	Actor, musician, artist, lecturer, producer, director, psychologist, spiritual teacher, politician, inventor.

MIND/BODY

Violets are dynamic, charismatic, visionary and powerful personalities. Their task or mission in life is to lead and inspire mankind and guide them into a new age of prosperity and wholeness. Most Violets have an inner and driving urge to do something important with their life.

Violets possess both knowledge and intuition. They also have the physical power and the resources necessary to make changes in their own or other peoples lives. Violets combine Blue and Red qualities on a new level of existence and vibration.

Violets are visionary, futuristic, and have high ideals and hopes for the future. They can usually see and recognize the "bigger picture" of any situation without being bogged down with details. They can literally see future incidents before their inner eyes.

They mainly perceive life through their "third eye" or "inner vision." Because they have the ability to visualize trends and future events they are often considered to be ahead of their time. Violets don't need to know details, facts and data to achieve or reach a goal.

They are more concerned with the bigger picture and the driving force behind it. Violets unorthodox and inventive ideas and uncanny perceptions often seem unrealistic and impractical to other people.

On the other hand, Violets are theoreticians. It is important to them that their ideas and projects work and make sense. Their vision allows them to see the cause or structure behind a technology, situation or event. Violets easily find the underlying laws and causes and intuitively know what steps to take.

A Violets motivation is to express and live their vision through artistic and innovative creativeness. The more they are able to fulfill their inner vision, the more content and happy they will be. The flexible Violet personality experiences life as magic and loves to be in a constant state of transformation and change.

Because Violet personalities integrate Blue and Red qualities it is important for them to accept and live various aspects of both. Those aspects and traits would include sensitivity, intuition, caring, love, compassion and physical activity, power, passion and strength. Violets usually have a strong, powerful physical body and excessive physical energy. They need to release their physical power through sports or other physical exercises. Because of their strong mind, relaxation in action is often a good outlet for letting go physically and mentally.

Violets have a charismatic and magnetic radiance. They possess an extremely emotional depth and exert a certain fascination over others. They know how to turn dreams into reality. Their state of mind is a magical place where wishes come true, a mystical union of subject and object. Most of the time they live in the future. They can extend their intuitive minds and sense what the future might hold or what trends might be successful. Violets are able to tune into an energy flow and intuitively sense where this river of energy is headed.

Violets love music more than nearly anything else. They feel the power and the vibration of music. However, they prefer energizing, quiet and harmonious music.

Music, which is destructive and negative, can irritate and frustrate a Violet and leave them in a strange condition. For Violets, music is the universal language, which connects humans and is also a powerful connection with the universe.

Violets are independent and need a lot of space for themselves. They need large apartments or houses with lots of open areas. Sometimes a castle is even too small for a Violets expansive energy field. They need this space intellectually as well as physically. They become impatient if they are caught in a small city or community when in fact they wish to be heard and expand their visions on a worldwide basis.

Violets may seem cold, aloof or unapproachable from the outside, but inside they are emotional, sensitive and filled with passion. They are careful with their emotions because they possess the sensitivity and depth of feelings of a Blue and the passion and energy of a Red. They are easily hurt and as a result use their cold exterior as a protective device. Giving others the impression of having self-esteem, strength and confidence does not necessarily mean they honestly feel that way. Violets often have doubts coupled with feelings of insecurity.

The largest challenge for a Violet personality is to trust their intuition and their inner vision. Their strong self-criticism and tendency toward perfection often leaves them with feelings of guilt and unworthiness. Part of a Violets mind always thinks they could do virtually anything better, faster and more efficiently. Even after completing a successful project they usually find small mistakes or details which they weren't able to see. This normally creates feelings of remorse.

Unbalanced Violets often ask themselves why they have such a strong feeling to do something important with their life. They wonder why they can't be like most other people without this burning urge to do or create something special. At the same time they feel unworthy or not good enough for the task. Successful and famous personalities, people who fulfill their goals and visions, are often confronted with these insecurities.

Out-of-power Violets can be arrogant, pompous and narcissistic. They think they are better than other people. An egotistical Violet can develop dictatorial attributes and truly basks in adoration and glory. Many out-of-power Violets do not trust their visions and ideas. They see too many possibilities and therefore become scattered, bewildered and confused. A common problem for out-of-power Violets is taking on too many projects at once and then trying to achieve the impossible. Being unrealistic, "too far out there," and not in touch with reality, can cause Violets to become frustrated and powerless.

If Violets have not found their vision and are not connected with their intuition, they often use their charismatic powers to achieve material wealth or high social status.   They have a tendency of compensating their missing spiritual connection with power, success and wealth.

Spirituality is an important concept for Violets. They see God in everything that exists. This is a universal or cosmic reality, not an Almighty God in the heavens. Violets understand that God is within all and we as human beings are co-creators of our own destiny. We are powerful, spiritual beings. Fulfilling their destiny means living a spiritual life. They understand living in this magical place of mind, where the universe takes care of them and provides them with everything they need.

SOCIAL LIFE

Violets often appear to be anti-social. They are far more interested in substantial or deep conversations or important projects and ideas than just hanging out with friends and talking about useless, unimportant subjects. Social interactions are boring and not necessary for them.

Violets are primarily involved in realizing their own visions and focusing on their own creativity. This often creates a distance between themselves and other people, including their own partners and friends.

It is important for Violets to come out of their cave every now and then, to have some fun, to enjoy the beauty life has to offer. They have to learn to let go of their vision, their attention, and focus on their "Third Eye" or vision center.

Violets have a strong, inner urge to support their community, their nation or the whole planet. They need to be in service to society in order to bring forth changes and improvements for society and mankind.

Violets can inspire and motivate society to seek new ways of creating a future which is in harmony, where humans can live without war, where the planet earth is understood as a living organism, where we are the creators of our own life and the masters of our own destiny. Violets teach humanity, that the universe will take care of us no matter what religion, belief or society we belong to or were born into. If we connect with the universal power, understand the flow of universal life energy, the "stuff" we are all made of, and if we align ourselves with the universe, we will be supported endlessly and without limits.

RELATIONSHIPS AND INTIMACY

While partnerships are important, they are not the first priority for most Violets. They need partners who can understand their visions, travel in similar directions and provide inspiration.

Violets love sexual excitement and are very passionate about it. They prefer "higher sex," where sexual union and orgasm is seen as a pathway to enlightenment, a male-female fusion, where duality ceases to exist. The sexual union represents a cosmic experience in which two beings of energy merge into one union.

Violets need sensual excitement and stimulation in their relationships. They are sensitive to their partners and immediately feel what type of thoughts they have toward them.

Violets can be both demanding and possessive in a relationship. They focus all their emotional attention on their mates. Because they merge so easily and completely with their lovers, they need to be aware of their own individuality and not get lost in a relationship. Violets have a tendency of being so totally consumed with their partners that they forget to maintain other friendships, even life long friendships.

If a Violets partner does not respond with equal passion and sensual intimacy, sexual problems can arise and frustration will certainly follow. Therefore, they should pay close attention to a balanced and satisfying love life.

Violets love the passion and power of Red people. You will feel the fire between them. If Violets accept and appreciate a Deep-Green they seem to be a good match for a successful and prosperous relationship. Violets need to understand that Orange personalities also need freedom and independence.

Yellow-Browns and Violets are good partners. They are very different yet support each other as a team. Violets with their dedication, drive and vision are opposite to a Yellows easy going and playful attitude. Blues love to be around Violets. They will be a loving and supportive partner.

Because Violets want to be the leader and are usually dominant in their relationships they need to make sure to pay enough attention to their partner. In general, Violets need partners who will support their vision and create a stimulating and passionate life together.

CAREER AND FINANCES

Violets have a need to be creative and express their visionary and innovative ideas. No matter what field of activity they are in, they will find new solutions that work more effectively.

Violets don't need much money for their private use. They enjoy the luxury it provides, but perceive money as representing power and influence. It gives them the ability to manifest and create their dreams and visions. Money gives them the freedom and power to make profound changes on this planet. Violets understand that in our society, you need to have money to be influential. But Violets are also careful with money. They tend to keep their finances together and are sometimes considered to be selfish and miserly.

Violets are born leaders. If they use their charismatic leadership abilities for the betterment of mankind and for humanitarian projects rather than egotistical purposes, other people will accept their powerful, autocratic and dictatorial style. It is difficult to resist the charisma and magical power of a Violet.

When in power, the universe seems to open all doors and supports Violets in a magical and effortless manner. They have an inner knowledge about the natural functions and laws of the universe. While many different color personalities have the perception that, "life is hard work," Violets teach us to trust our inner flow and that the universe will take care of us all the time. If we are connected to our Universal Life Energy, life manifests itself without effort.

Violets are highly intelligent and have the ability to look deeply into situations and problems. They are always looking for laws or patterns and through their analytical thinking are able to find the causes behind things. As a result of their ability to examine most situations mentally and emotionally, and their intuitive and creative expression, they are creative and innovative problem solvers.

Violets normally tend to choose occupations, which allow them independence or creative freedom. They believe strongly in the purpose of their activity and must see a higher purpose in what they are doing. Violets are often drawn to the entertainment industry, the media or, the field of communications because of their magnetic charisma and personality. They know how to use the existing tools to make valuable and important changes on this planet and get their message across.

Other areas in which Violets are often involved include, philosophy, religion, ecology, music, literature, art and humanitarian, futuristic technologies, projects and developments.

Typical "Violet" occupations are: Actor, musician, artist, author, lecturer, designer, producer, director, photographer, psychologist, social-worker, spiritual teacher, politician, business owner and inventor.

HEALTH, WELL-BEING AND GROWTH

If Violet personalities learn to focus their energy, believe and trust in their vision, and stay grounded in reality, they can achieve anything. Living out their visions with passion in their heart will always guide them in the right direction.

Violets cannot be ordered to restrict their visions. However, it is important for them to only concentrate on a few projects at any given time. Making clear plans, organizing their day and their life, will help them find their real goals and vision. After they are clear in knowing what they want they need to finish one project after the other without changing plans to often.

Violets feel an inner tension, something, which drives them forward to find and fulfill their innermost visions. They will not be happy if they continually resist this inner urge of living out their mission and their dreams.

Violets need to confront themselves with their guilt and their unworthiness. If they understand their vision and are connected to the universe, they will let go of their guilt and focus on their wonderful and promising future.

It is important for Violets to have time for themselves to focus and meditate. This helps them come into contact with their inner visions.

Deep meditations which connect them with the universal life energy flow, tantra, yoga exercises, listening to harmonious, energizing music are important tools for Violets to remain centered. Wearing or surrounding themselves with the color violet can help them to become more centered and powerful. Violets should pay close attention to their sex and love life. Finding a passionate, loving and supportive partner is essential for their success.

Violets have a tremendous passion for life. If this flow of energy is intact they will be in power. Violets need to experience that the universe is full of energy and once they are connected to the universal life energy they will receive an unlimited supply.

If Violets find their place in the universe, understand the role they have to play in this great cosmic production, and feel this inner connection with the universal power, they will be supported limitlessly. Violets always seem to have luck. It often appears that they don't need to work very hard for their success. But in reality, their success is the outward manifestation of their harmony with the universe. For a Violet, life is magic.

LAVENDER PERSONALITIES

The following are the qualities and action words associated with LAVENDER personalities:

Area	Description
Physical	Fragile, weak physical body, look like angels or fairies, pale skin, artistic, often ungrounded or unrealistic, dreamland.
Emotional	Sensitive, enchantment, insecure, aloof, live in their own dream world, don't like confrontations and harsh reality.
Mental	Imaginative, artistic, creative thinkers, visionary, idealistic, ideals and intuitions, fantasy, dreams, visualization.
Spiritual	Mystical, higher dimensions, meditative state, angels, fairies.
Motivation	Experiencing dreams and fantasies, mental and spiritual creative.
Mission/ Vision	Express their imagination and dreams into physical reality.
Growth	Uncontrolled, imaginative, from inside out.
Exercise	Grounding exercises, Qui Gong, gardening, walking, nature.
Recharge battery	Connect with spiritual energy, creative expressions, like painting.
Communication	Strong inner communication, contact with inner worlds, higher dimensional beings, fantasy figures, angels.
Interaction	Unpredictable, follow their inner clock, unstructured, spontaneous.
Relationships	Loners, need freedom, mainly relationship with inner world, social.
Social, Friends	Unconventional, few close friends.
Sex, Intimacy	Creative, light, experimental, transcendent.
Money	Security, unreal concept, difficult to handle.

MIND/BODY

Lavenders prefer living in their own fantasy and dream world. Enchantment, myths, inner "higher" dimensions of existence, angels and fairies are all concepts, which fill a Lavenders mind. They spend most of their time out of their bodies in a world of imagination.

Lavenders are mentally free to explore new possibilities, concepts and realities. Their minds function without any limitations. Whatever they can imagine is possible and real. This unique ability allows them to produce new, creative and often "far out" ideas. Lavenders believe in "Life is a fantasy land, where dreams come true."

Lavenders can perceive energies through their unique and sensitive inner senses. Many Lavenders have the ability able to "see" other dimensions and worlds and experience other realities. This allows them to communicate with higher dimensions and perceive ideas, concepts and imaginations far beyond most people's understanding. They also have access to spiritual and etheric energies, which they might use for healing.

These fantasy-oriented personalities enjoy soft, meditative music, wind chimes, candles, incense, meditation and the rhythmic sounds of chanting. They enjoy any sound, color, texture or environment, which can inspire their imaginations, help them leave their bodies or help them move toward an etheric state of mind.

Lavenders can be entertaining as well as educational. With their colorful imagination and higher perception they can guide us into a land of fantasy and enchantment. In power Lavenders are wonderful storytellers, writers or artists. They have the talent to describe and visualize worlds of magic and mystical places where spirits and fairies reside.

Lavenders can take us beyond our limited, harsh reality into a world filled with possibilities. They need to be free without physical, emotional or mental limitations. They need to fly with the wind, to be able to change into any direction at their own will.

They feel an urge and a pull to experience their inner dimensions. They feel that their intuition and inner guidance, which they sometimes refer to as "guardian angel," will support them on their way.

Lavenders see life as a magical world of adventure, filled with fairies, spirits, angels and other "unreal" phenomena. They are here to stimulate humanities imagination, to inspire our sense of wonder and keep the idea of magic alive in us all.

Lavenders do not have strong physical bodies. As a result of living more in their inner world then in physical reality, they dislike being confronted with reality. Physical reality, as most people perceive it, seems cold, harsh, even brutal. Therefor they seek environments or situations where life is light, easy, pretty and enchanting.

Lavenders don't have the same concept of reality as most other people. In their mind and their fantasy they can produce and create any form of reality. To them this imaginative reality is an existing plane where dreams come true. Our beliefs, thoughts and imaginations play a vital role in creating our physical reality. "Energy follows thought," is one of the fundamental rules in human cosmology. Lavender personalities understand this concept and are able to use their imaginations and thoughts to create and change realities.

When in power, Lavenders can use their creative talents to show people the unlimited possibilities of other realms. They have the ability to transform their visions into works of art, which can enhance the lives of their fellow beings. They need to be with people who can see the potential in their ideas and are capable of forming plans and taking action with them. Lavenders are able to inspire and stimulate other color personalities to produce new and futuristic, sometimes unreal products and ideas.

Lavenders live by their feelings and intuition, rather than by their intellect. They have a very intuitive and creative way of thinking. They have difficulty processing analytical, rigid and structured concepts or beliefs. They want to be free to explore their imaginations and experience other realities.

Lavenders physical bodies are sensitive, fragile and frail and their physical appearance is often weak and pale. They have no interest or plans for physical activities such as hard work or even sports. Staying in their mental, intuitive fantasyland is often enough by itself.

Lavenders are sensitive beings. Their soft and fragile physical bodies aren't capable of dealing with many real life situations. Their inner senses of higher sensory perception can be overloaded easily. Therefore, Lavenders need to be aware of their sensitive nervous system and take appropriate precautions.

They need to organize their environment to the point of finding peace and harmony. When that is accomplished they will be able to stay in contact with higher dimensions and will also be powerful communicators, teaching us about the land of fantasy and imagination. If Lavenders stay grounded in physical reality and have a good contact with their physical body, they are powerful spiritual beings using the art of imagination and visualization.

Lavenders who are out of power prefer daydreaming and escaping reality. As a result of spending most of their time living in another world, it is difficult for them to describe their experiences and imaginations. Unbalanced Lavenders cannot bring back their dreams and share them with their friends. They keep their inner world and stories to themselves because they do not feel the need for expression. They are forgetful and scattered. Their visions and ideas seem unrealistic and illusionary to most other people.

Because they have a hard time differentiating between fantasy and reality, they have a tendency of being spacy and forgetful. Many people, on a regular basis, tell Lavenders that they are completely unrealistic. If a friend of yours often seems to be spacy and just not present, not quite in tune with reality, it is likely he is in a Lavender state of mind.

Most out-of-power Lavenders have difficulty functioning in the real world. They don't like dealing with day-to-day business activities such as paying their bills, shopping or meeting many people.

However, they often require others to support them. They can be like frightened rabbits, running into another dimension to escape this "hard" reality called life.

Many unbalanced Lavenders float in a land between reality and dream. They have strange ideas and perceptions about life. They need to be aware of the difference between the different planes of existence. Physical reality functions through scientific laws, which cannot be overcome or overridden by imagination or dreaming. However, in their world of fantasy, these laws might not be valid and anything continues to be possible.

Lavenders are able to visualize or imagine what God might look like. They have access to higher dimensions where reality takes on many different forms and structures. If they learn to stay grounded and focused, they will experience and communicate with God. As a result, Lavenders are good spiritual teachers and are able to support and help others in their personal and spiritual growth.

When Lavenders find their spiritual purpose and connection, they can become psychic counselors and therapists. They are free thinkers. They do not wish to be involved in any rigid, spiritual or religious belief or philosophy. Even if they search for spiritual practices and groups, they rarely connect with them on a deeper level.

SOCIAL LIFE

On one hand, Lavenders are well liked by society because they are stimulating, creative and filled with wonder and imagination. They are especially accepted and appreciated if they find themselves in artistic or performing professions. On the other hand, Lavenders are sometimes irresponsible, unreliable and difficult to be around.

They have a tendency of being forgetful and they also have bad memories. Lavenders will forget appointments or decide to change their plans without giving notice to their partners or friends.

It is common behavior for a Lavender to get up from their chair, go into another room, and then recognize they have forgotten why. Or, they drive their car for ten minutes without noticing where they are going. Many friends, partners and associates cannot get used to this unpredictable behavior. Lavenders often feel guilty or inadequate because they are aware of their unorthodox and sometimes unconventional behavior.

Most out-of-power Lavenders try to adjust to societies rules and regulations. But they must understand that by adjusting to what they consider to be societies illusion, and not following their own intuition and guidance, will leave them with feelings of unhappiness and sadness. Their mind and their imagination are always free and cannot be trapped or caught up into a small and limited reality.

RELATIONSHIPS AND INTIMACY

Lavenders need strong and understanding partners in their relationships. Because Lavenders have difficulty with reality and are not very grounded, they have a hard time offering any sort of stability to a relationship. If they are treated with gentleness and kindness they will in turn be gracious, sensitive, appreciative and dedicated mates.

At first, their mates are attracted to and fascinated by the imaginative Lavenders. However, most of those mates quickly learn that they are living with a fragile and sensitive butterfly who is sometimes present and sometimes not. Their loved ones can eventually find the Lavenders innocence and creative imagination both endearing and lovable.

Lavenders do not necessarily need the closeness of others. Nor do they need emotional or social nurturing from friends or family. They need enough space around them, without restrictions or obligations, to give them the freedom to live in their own world. Relationships are not a primary issue because living in their dream and fantasy world is quite fulfilling.

Lavenders are experimental and creative in lovemaking and like to fantasize during sex. They often leave their bodies and drift into other dimensions. Making love can be a spiritual and etheric experience for them. If a Lavenders partner is sensitive, caring and playful, they will enjoy sex and return much love to their partner.

Because of their fragile physical and emotional system, Lavenders are often careful with their sexuality. It is a very intense and powerful experience and can easily create emotional traumas. On the other side to stay centered they need to understand the importance of relationships, sexuality and their physical, emotional body.

A healthy sex life will allow them to feel their physical body but still be connected with their dream and fantasy world. Relationships are a wonderful mirror for Lavenders. They reflect their ability to stay centered and grounded in physical reality.

Lavenders might be attracted to all physical color types but in reality they will have difficulties in creating a lasting relationship. Reds, Deep-Reds, Orange and Yellow personalities are doers; they want to be physical active and creative.

But a Lavender feels more comfortable exploring ideas in their own mind. Physical action is way too much work. Yellow-Browns are too realistic and mental for the imaginative and artistic Lavender.

Lavenders love the playfulness of Yellow personalities. Greens and Deep- Greens enjoy communicating with Lavenders and like their mental activity and vivid imagination. Blues and Lavenders generally make a good match but occasionally lack the direction and strength to make a relationship work. Violets and Whites have a lot in common with the imaginative and spiritual oriented Lavender personality.

If Lavenders find enough freedom and support in a relationship they will be loving and creative partners.

CAREER AND FINANCES

Lavenders will be found wherever creative imagination, fantasy and free thinking are needed. As writers, actors or artists they are free to explore their creativity and produce their fantasy and dreams into reality. Through their visual and imaginative styles they have the unique ability to take people into a fantasy world which is alive with feelings, sensations and sounds. In healing and therapy, Lavenders are able to use both their psychic and spiritual experiences and their knowledge of the mind and the inner worlds to help and support others.

Lavenders solve their problems by being creative and inventive. Because they are imaginative and inventive they sometimes come up with unorthodox and unrealistic solutions. However, they often need others to finish the job. They are perfect in finding creative solutions but are often too etheric to do physical work. They don't like to get their hands dirty.

When Lavenders are out of power they don't want to confront themselves with problems at all. They escape into their fantasy world and simply wish to not be bothered. Lavenders are creative and intuitive problem solvers but too much mental work, thinking and analyzing can easily overload their sensitive system.

Lavenders have difficulty in dealing with the physical reality of money. They are not good at earning money but when they do it is usually spent just as quickly. They like to be supported by others but still must confront themselves with the day-to-day reality of making a living and creating prosperity. Lavenders need to learn to bring their imagination and focus into the handling of their financial situations.

Lavenders do not like positions of leadership or occupations, which involve demanding, hard and stressful work. They are pleasant and friendly and work best in low stress, quiet environments. They do not prefer regular, office jobs or analytical, mental occupations. They should find activities where they can integrate their creative imagination and fantasies.

Typical "Lavender" occupations are: Storyteller, artist, writer, mime, actor, dancer, designer, decorator, teacher, dreamer, spiritual teacher or healer

HEALTH, WELL-BEING AND GROWTH

To stay in power, Lavenders need to understand the importance of physical reality. We were born on this planet to experience and learn to live within a three dimensional, physical world. As long as they are courageous enough to face the real world and to stay in their bodies they will live a joyous and imaginative life. They have a need to explore and live out their fantasies and imaginations, but they also need to live and express their visions in the real world.

Lavenders need to escape into their dream world for the same reason most people need to sleep. They need time to relax so that they are free to dream, fantasize and play with their imaginations. It helps them unwind and recuperate from the stress of the world. Creating a peaceful environment where they are free to spend lots of time to think, imagine and create new dream and fantasy worlds is essential for Lavenders.

Meditation and visualization are familiar concepts to them. But they also need to confront themselves with their personal power, their ability to express and live their own creativity, and their own strength. The more Lavenders are able to ground themselves, the more they will make their ideas and imaginations a reality.

Lavenders are not very attached to their bodies. Because they have a tendency of being so ungrounded, they need to take care of their physical temple on a regular basis. Physical exercise, such as walking, gardening, connecting with the soil, swimming and other subtle forms of physical activity, will help Lavenders stay in contact with their body. Staying grounded in their physical body means also a healthy life.

To create balance they need to live consciously in their imaginations. But they also need to come back into their bodies and into reality. Using imagination for healing is a powerful tool for Lavenders to heal both themselves and others.

Lavenders love creating a "holy and divine" atmosphere and space with incense, candles, lights, colors and music to support their experience of imagination, inspiration and spiritual insights.

As long as Lavenders use their ability of seeing other dimensions and worlds and use their imaginative thinking to create new ideas, concepts and forms, they will be happy and content and will have a supportive and helping influence on our planet.

WHITE PERSONALITIES

The following are the qualities and action words associated with WHITE personalities:

Area	Description
Physical	Delicate, sensitive, fragile physical bodies, need lots of physical, private space, radiate lightness, brightness, transcendence.
Emotional	Sensitive, emotional chameleons, difficult to set boundaries, overwhelming and over powering emotions, healing and light.
Mental	Intuitive, bright, learning, conservative, adjust to their environment.
Spiritual	Transcendental, cosmic, healing power, higher dimensions of existence, meditation, high vibration, healing state of mind.
Motivation	By inner peace, connection with Spirit-God.
Mission/ Vision	Teach healing and spirituality, channel healing energy.
Growth	Cosmic flow, transcendent unity, connect to God source.
Exercise	Yoga, Qi Gong, Tai Chi, Meditation.
Recharge battery	Meditation, visualization, tuning into cosmic energy, spiritual force.
Communication	Silent, soft, transcendental-spiritual values.
Interaction	One-to-one or small groups, can tune into people very easily, takes on other qualities.
Relationships	Strong God relationship, loners, soul-to-soul connections, spiritual values and belief determine friends and partners.
Social, Friends	Shy, withdrawn, only a few close friends.
Sex, Intimacy	Transcendental, tantric sexuality, careful in mixing energies with others, too sensitive and open, enlightening experience.

Money	Security, secondary, careful in spending.
Success	To heal, teach and enlighten humanity.
Occupation	Work alone, quiet environment, with like minded people.
Career	Healer, spiritual counselor, healing and teaching professions.

MIND/BODY

Spirituality, transcendence and cosmic, universal concepts are familiar to White personalities. They are closer to God than all other color personalities. They almost make an impression of being mirrors, or channels of divine and spiritual qualities, living in this physical reality. Whites reflect the highest vibration of energy: White light, the universal life force. White, or crystal light, is actually itself not a color. It is the quintessence of all colors of the rainbow or all colors combined.

A Whites motivation is based on how clear they feel inside and how much healing energy they can channel through their bodies. They perceive life like a mirror, which reflects and shows who they are and how much light-energy they are able to integrate. Being connected with their inner, spiritual, divine force and functioning as a healing channel are also motivations for a White.

They are guided by their higher mind to show humanity what powerful, spiritual beings humans are. Spirit or God is the essence of life itself.

Whites have a tendency of being quiet but quick thinkers. Their highly developed mind functions on an intuitive and spiritual basis rather than an analytical basis. Whites are also fast learners. They can tune into information or knowledge easily because they are like a prism or an empty glass.

They love to read books, watch movies, attend the theater or other social events, which inspires them to more clearly understand the meaning of life.

On the other hand, Whites enjoy spending time by themselves. They need to regularly withdraw from their environment in order to contemplate life and spirituality. White personalities are channels for universal healing energy. They are natural healers and find great joy in helping other people with their own healing process. As a result of having clear energy themselves, they are able to channel high vibrational healing energy through their bodies.

Whites are able to keep their thoughts and emotions out of the way.   They have access to transcendental states of consciousness, where matter and reason have no place. It feels natural for Whites to connect with inner dimensions of existence. To them, these higher vibrational planes are as substantial and "real" as physical reality. They know that we as human beings live in a world of limitations. Our spirit is free and will live forever.

Whites are like glass prisms. The purity of the material determines how much light will actually shine through. The more clear the channel or medium is, the more powerful the healing life energy can flow through it. Consciousness and awareness are the most powerful tools for a White personality.

Whites reflect all energy qualities on a higher level and therefore can easily transform themselves. They have the unique ability of transforming and tuning themselves into other situations or other people's mind, body and spirit. Whites, with their clear-white energy, are energetic chameleons and therefore easily take on the characteristics, behavioral patterns, emotions and thoughts of other people. They can change their vibrations just like tuning a piano.

Conscious Whites use this ability to understand and heal themselves and others. Unconscious Whites tend to absorb or take in other people's life energy colors. Some people might feel an energy drain when they are around a Whites energy field.

Whites usually don't realize that they take on other people's personality traits or characters. They suddenly begin to behave like the person they are talking with, to the point of knowing the other person's feelings or even knowing their thoughts. In power Whites can use this ability to tune into their patients to find our more about their psycho-emotional problems.

Whites are physically fragile and delicate. They like to create and then live in a pretty, clean and gentle environment. They function best if they live in an uncluttered, quiet and orderly atmosphere.

Whites need a great deal of time and space for themselves to meditate, reflect, nurture and balance themselves. It is as if they need to clean and recharge their own life energy batteries on a regular basis. As soon as their system is overloaded or damaged they will withdraw, go within themselves to recharge and clean. Just like a White, clear river that has been polluted, they know how to clean their energy stream.

Whites try to avoid harsh, loud, heartless, insensitive and disharmonious environments because they don't know how to interact with physical reality. All kinds of disturbances or stresses, whether physical, emotional or mental, are damaging to their inner balance. Because they are so sensitive and receptive, they need a lot of time to recharge themselves. Spirituality, healing and peacefulness are far more important to them than creating physical ideas or working on projects and achieving success.

Whites are ultimately striving for enlightenment, the state of consciousness in which duality, time and space cease to exist. They are seeking a state of no-mind or super-mind, where they can be one with the universe. Being quiet and pure inside allows them to have a true and deep connection with the Source, or God.

They live their lives through intuition and inner guidance in a state of transcendence or heightened awareness. They also teach humanity the importance of transcendence and the existence of a powerful spiritual, divine cosmic energy.

In power Whites are quiet, sensitive and peaceful individuals. If they stay centered they experience inner peace and harmony and radiate this enlightened feeling toward others. They vibrate at a very high level and sometimes, just to stay in their White clear energy field, can heal other people around them.

Whites teach humanity that healing can take place if we allow spirit or God to do the work. We cannot force our own development or healing. Real healing and spiritual growth can only occur when God is present.

If out of power, Whites can become disoriented and depressed. If they don't follow their intuitions and are not in tune with their spirit, they become confused and scattered. Not being connected with their life purpose and their clear healing energy, they tend to give up and shut themselves off from life.

Whites often lack self-confidence and are constantly looking for reassurance and approval from others. Being sensitive and easily hurt they often retreat inside to be alone with their emotions. They are often insecure about making decisions and dependent on others to run their lives. They normally don't like large crowds. If Whites are out of power they tend to adapt behaviors and responses from others. When this occurs they also forget what their real purpose on this planet is.

White personalities have an inner connection and an urge to live and experience God. They are closer to God and have a wider awareness then most other color personalities. Whites don't think, feel or discuss God or Spirit. They experience it. They feel, and know, that God is in everything alive, from the smallest atom to the largest star. It is their belief that we are God, powerful spiritual beings.

SOCIAL LIFE

White personalities are usually cautious in their interactions with other people. However, they do have close friends whom they trust. Choosing their friends on a spiritual and soul-to-soul basis ensures a safe and peaceful environment.

They are flexible enough to live in and with society, but they usually need a considerable amount of time and space for themselves.

Their strong God connection allows them to stay alone for long periods of time. If they are in contact with their Inner Light, their Higher Self, they don't need to be surrounded by people. On the other hand, Whites want to share their light and healing energies and bring peace, healing and enlightenment to all of society. They are often found as reverends, counselors and teachers in spiritual organizations or churches.

Whites know that we are all interconnected and beings of light. This knowledge helps them channel their light energy into this physical reality and also facilitate healing and peace. Whites primarily live and work on higher dimensions of existence.

White personalities do not feel the need to be accepted by society. If they are in an unbalanced state they will try to get other peoples attention and use this attention as a substitute for their lost inner connection with the spirit/light. In power Whites might be very sensitive beings but they still have abundant healing energy available

RELATIONSHIPS AND INTIMACY

Whites are fragile and sensitive beings. They need their own special space much more than a social life or close relationships. They only allow close friends, partners or associates to become emotionally and even physically close. Dependent on their clarity and healing power, Whites love the process of helping and healing others.

Even so, this does not indicate they are open for intimate relationships. In working situations they prefer small groups or one-to-one relationships. This gives them the opportunity to focus, concentrate and tune completely into one person. Large crowds have a tendency of disturbing them, creating imbalances, and do not allow them to stay in contact with their clear, transcendent energies.

Whites are primarily loners because their inner connection with God is enough by itself. No one can compete with God as his or her source of inspiration and peace.

Whites are careful and often choose a conservative approach to their relationships. If they are able to stay in power they can have a very healing, peaceful and spiritual effect on their partner. But their mate needs to understand that Whites must clear themselves regularly from disharmonious energies and find their own purpose in life, which means, creating a healing and peaceful environment both within and around them.

Sexuality for Whites is a divine, spiritual experience. It creates a connection with the universal life energy. During orgasm Whites melt with and even become God. But Whites do not need sex or physical love. Their expanded perception of love comes from their ability to connect with higher dimensions. Love and compassion has nothing to do with emotional feelings or physical behavior. Unconditional love means sharing healing and love energy. Love is the essence of life itself.

Whites enjoy making love but they need a safe, caring and strong partner who understands their sensitive nature. Because they interact so intensely with other people, making love can be an emotionally intense and sometimes disturbing experience. Whites can remain single or celibate for long periods of time.

Lavenders and Violets have similarities in that both of them need a lot of time to recharge themselves and connect with God. Lavenders and Blues often experience difficulties in finding intimacy and common ground. Indigos and Whites can create a powerful spiritual relationship based on love and understanding.

Greens seem to understand and support a Whites needs, whereas Yellow-Browns tend to be too mental and regularly withdraw and isolate themselves.

Even if Whites could learn a lot from being together with all physical color personalities this doesn't happen very often. Reds and Oranges are just too intense and physical to be compatible with Whites. Deep-Reds do not have the same concept of life and spirituality. Yellows are too extroverted, playful and active to create a lasting relationship with a White person.

In their relationships, Whites need a lot of space for themselves. They need partners who can give them this space and also support them in their need to find inner peace and enlightenment.

CAREER AND FINANCES

Making money and taking care of physical demands is not a main issue for White personalities. They can exist on the physical plane but live most the time in their spiritual world. It is a good idea for them to let others handle their financial matters so they can be free for their healing and spiritual work. Whites handle money with care because it represents security. They take very few risks and try maintain a lifestyle, which is easy, clean and simple.

Whites judge their work and their success by how calm and peaceful they feel and by how clear and effective their healings are. Their greatest reward is being connected to the Universal Source/God.

To solve their problems Whites need to trust their intuition and to allow the healing energy to flow through them. While solving their problems they are cautious and tend to lean toward old, proven solutions. Whites bodies are sensitive and fragile. As a result they need a peaceful and meditative environment to tap into their power and use their gifts of healing and teaching.

Typical "White" occupations are: Healer, therapist, spiritual teacher, nun, monk, secretary, librarian, receptionist, artist and enlightened master.

HEALTH, WELL-BEING AND GROWTH

Whites will be in a healthy and balanced state if they are connected with their life purpose. To stay in power they must learn to go within. They need to live in a transcendent state of consciousness. Living every second in a state of heightened awareness is exactly what their soul is looking for. Once they understand their purpose in life, and once they learn to maintain a high energy level, they will be happy and content personalities.

White personalities need to communicate with Spirit and God on a regular basis. They must constantly retreat to their own environment in order to clean their own life energy. This will help them in staying centered and clear, to remain an open channel for the clear, high vibrational healing energy. Surrounding themselves with nature, growing flowers or planting gardens is highly therapeutic. It also supports them toward finding greater inner peace and harmony.

Whites bodies are sensitive and fragile. It is essential to their health that they connect with their inner healing energy and become a crystal-clear channel of life energy. A Whites healing ability can be compared with an electrical lightning system. The more energy flows through the system, the more light will shine. If the electrical system is clear and without blockages, the healing light energy will radiantly flow. The more light a White is able to generate, the more powerful and healthy they will be.

Whites easily take on other people's energies. They have to regenerate and rejuvenate themselves on a regular basis in a peaceful and meditative environment. Inasmuch as they pick up other people's emotions, thoughts and personality traits, they need to stay centered and strong in their interactions with other humans. Recharging their life energy batteries on a regular basis and having enough space and time for themselves is essential for a healthy and empowering life.

Transcendental or light meditation techniques are wonderful ways for Whites to connect with Spirit and their healing power. Once they are in contact with their source they will be guided in their daily life and in their healings.

White personalities understand the concept of "give and you shall receive." Their strong healing power and ability to be a channel of clear life energy gives them the skill to send and share this healing force with others. They know that giving others our love and attention will create a healing and growth process from within.

Sending warm and heartfelt feelings and thoughts to friends and close ones will heal them and help them find their way. Healing occurs first in the spiritual realm and then continues in our mind and body.

Whites largest gift to humanity is to demonstrate and live their clear healing abilities and to show that we are energy. The moment we focus on healing and growth it will happen and manifest in our life.

AURA VIDEO STATION

Did you find "your" Aura Color Personality? Or did you see yourself reflected in several of the Aura Color Types? Then the next step is to look at your current State of Energy - your Aura.

At this stage of AURA MASTERY the Inneractive Aura Video technology comes into play. Measuring and monitoring your "real" state of mind/body and energy can give you valuable feedback about yourself and your future journey of exploration.

First, it will confirm your real Aura Color Type and second, it will show you that you are capable of expressing more then just one aura color. It will reflect your ability to radiate the whole rainbow spectrum of colors. You are a being of light and energy, which is capable of living all colors of the rainbow.

Now, it is time to look at your personal aura colors through the AURA VIDEO STATION ™.

Just imagine the following situation: You sit in front of the AURA VIDEO STATION, slide your hand into the futuristic looking Bio Sensor or Bio Glove™ and magically your vibrating, colorful Aura appears on the screen. You see your face, your body and your aura colors on the screen and with amazement you realize how beautiful and radiant you really are.

Just by watching your aura colors pulsate and vibrate you understand that you are much more then you have imagined. Seeing your energy field change in real-time according to your emotional, mental or energetic responses and patterns is an experience by itself.

It is impossible to explain the experience of actually seeing your Aura - live - on a PC or TV screen. Try for yourself and you will see.

AURA MASTERY 7

Find an Inneractive AURA VIDEO STATION in your area. After the AVS-operator has hooked you up with the Bio Sensor your personal Aura Colors will appear on the screen.

Now, it is time to prepare yourself for your first **AURA MASTERY** exercise with the AURA VIDEO STATION:

While your watch your own Aura Color on the AURA VIDEO STATION monitor allow yourself to relax for a few minutes. Take a few deep breaths and let go of your daily stress. With every minute you relax and slowly go back to your personal space and energy.

In this exercise you will learn to monitor your inner changes through the Aura Video on the screen. Watch your Aura Colors - especially the changes that occur. You always should remember: Every movement and change you see reflects your physical, emotional, mental and spiritual state.

The first step towards AURA MASTERY is to recognize your current state of energy. Pay attention to the dominant Aura Color on the screen.

What is your base vibration? Do you radiate in a physical, energetic, creative red-orange-yellow? Do you express a balanced, communicative and harmonious green-blue or an intuitive, spiritual, calm indigo-violet-white Aura?

Green indicates the middle, balance and harmony, all rainbow colors towards Red show more physical energy, excitement and activity. All colors towards Violet indicate heightened awareness and sensitivity, low physical energy and excitement.

Relax your mind and feel your own Aura Colors. Open your heart and feel what each color has to tell you. Like a good movie your Aura can show you the way toward a better, healthier and more successful life.

Next, watch the changes within your Aura. Is your Aura very calm and harmonious or very excited and active? Do you see only one color or combinations of Aura Colors?

After you have familiarized yourself with your current state of energy and you also understand what your Aura Colors indicate, try the following experiment:

Think and feel of a certain situation in your life where you felt very angry or upset. The more intense, the better. Feel the energy in your belly, tune yourself completely into this situation.

Don't be surprised if your Aura Colors have changed already. Did you activate more red emotional and excitement energy or did you withdraw into more blue and violet?

Now, think and feel of a pleasant, loving and relaxing situation in your life. Feel completely a person you love or tune into a healing or relaxing feeling. I know you will enjoy the effects and results.

The real challenge of AURA MASTERY is to change your Aura Colors through the power of your mind. You are the master, it is up to you to change the energy around you. If you change your Aura, your life will change and improve accordingly.

Feel free to use any technique or tools that will help you to become an AURA MASTER. Experiment with your favorite healing, relaxation or meditation technique, massage, Reiki hands on healing, Crystals and gemstones, magnets, music, color therapy products and watch the effects of these tools on your Aura.

At any time feel free to ask the trained personal to assist you during your AURA MASTERY session. You might even get a professional Aura reading from your counselor.

Remember, once you can create all rainbow colors in your Aura then you are an AURA MASTER. Then you know that you are a powerful being of energy without any limitations.

❤ *Accept the challenge to be an AURA MASTER.* ❤

AURA MASTERY TEST

Ask yourself the following questions and determine what areas in your life are "low energies or vibes" and which activities will help you in creating a higher level of energy and vibration.

Before you begin you might want to create a relaxing and meditative environment. Allow yourself plenty of time for each question. Start with the first question and make a list with your answers. You can use a separate sheet for each question.

Over the next few weeks pay close attention to your daily life. Whenever you notice something important write it down.

■ **INCREASE YOUR ENERGY**

How do my business and private relationships effect me? Are they recharging or depleting my inner batteries?

....
....
....
....
....
....

Do I live in an environment, which is energizing for me or do my surroundings take energy away from me?

....
....
....
....
....
....
....

What creates stress or tensions and needs to be changed?

....
....
....
....
....
....

What activities, relationships and life situations drain my energies and need to be changed or eliminated?

....
....
....
....
....
....

Do you feel energized living in your apartment or home? How can you create your "High Energy Home?

....
....
....
....
....
....

What kind of physical, mental or spiritual exercises or activities make me feel energetic and powerful?

....
....
....
....
....
....

■ **RAISE YOUR VIBRATION**

What in your life do you see as beautiful, loving and radiant?

....
....
....
....
....
....

When do you feel totally happy, harmonious and satisfied?

....
....
....
....
....
....

What creates an uplifted, deeply satisfying feeling of love and enlightenment inside you?

....
....
....
....
....
....

What is your dream come true? How would your "perfect" life look like?

....
....
....
....
....
....

Is there anything in your life where you hold on to and feel you should let go of it?

....
....
....
....
....
....

What feels dark, uncomfortable or bad to you? What in your life feels like "low vibes" and need to be changed?

....
....
....
....
....
....

What techniques do you practice daily to raise your vibration and to create a higher state of awareness?

....
....
....
....
....
....

If you are interested in continuing your journey please contact Inneractive for upcoming AURA MASTERY lectures and seminars.

AURA IMAGING PHOTOGRAPHY
Written by Johannes R. Fisslinger

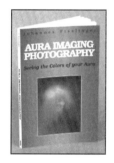

This excellent book will enlighten you on the subject of Aura Photography. *Johannes R. Fisslinger* will guide you into the world of auras and energy.

Understand the scientific principals of Aura Imaging technology, the human aura and biofeedback. Includes 30 colorful Aura Photos with detailed aura color analysis.

SUM PRESS * ISBN 0-9629352-3-9

MAGICAL AURAS
Written by Bettina Bernoth-Fisslinger

What aura colors do Dannion Brinkley, Timothy Leary, Dr. Fred Bell or Johannes R. Fisslinger have?

This easy-to-read book from *Bettina Bernoth* includes many celebrity aura photos and will help you to interpret your own aura colors.

SUM PRESS * ISBN 0-9629352-8-X

Ask your local bookstore, healing center or contact Inneractive Company directly for an **Inneractive AURA VIDEO STATION** in your area or for other **AURAMASTERY** products.

If you are interested in using the AURA VIDEO STATION as a therapy, healing, educational tool or as a # 1 business opportunity, please contact:

inneractive

520 Washington Blvd. # 907 • Marina del Rey, CA 90292
Phone 310-390-7090 • Fax 310-390-8167
E-Mail aura@inneractive.com

Visit our web site: http://www.inneractive.com